Corporates are from Mars,
Charities are from Venus.

"The imperative to deliver successful cross sector partnerships has rarely been greater. This is a very practical book, a must read for charities and corporates alike."

DAVID THOMLINSON
Senior Managing Director - Geographic Strategy & Operations. Accenture

"This excellent best practice guide welcomes a new spirit of collaborations between business and the voluntary sector – a mutually supportive partnership which I hope will deliver increasingly creative solutions for the sector."

NICK HURD MP
Minister for Civil Society

"Never has increased collaboration and partnerships between the corporate and voluntary sectors been of greater importance. This book provides a well researched, easily accessible and practical guide to those in the corporate world and the charity sector. It should be read by everyone who wishes to understand the potential benefits that they and the wider national economy can enjoy if they become actively involved in CR initiatives. It is an important contribution to a vital subject."

BARONESS GREENGROSS OF NOTTING HILL

Corporates are from Mars, *Charities are from Venus.*

The ultimate guide to managing your partnership.

Kay Allen
with
Tanja Rasmussen

Published in the United Kingdom 2012

British Library Cataloging in Publication Data. A catalogue record for this book is available from the British Library.

ISBN 978-0-9547059-1-6

Designed by Jonathan Madden

Typeset in Garamond and Din

Produced by CST The Gate cstthegate.com

Printed by Pegasus Colour Print Limited

FOREWORD
BY ALAN COOK, CBE

Alan is Chairman of Action for M.E. He is also Chairman of the University of Bedfordshire, the Highways Agency, Irish Life and Permanent Group Holdings Plc, based in Dublin where he now works two days per week, and is a Non-Executive Director of Sainsbury's Bank. Alan has spent most of his career in financial services and his most recent executive roles were as Chief Executive of National Savings and Investments and Managing Director of Post Office Ltd.

Alan's daughter, Jenny, has M.E.

With cut-backs taking place in every walk of life, both public, private and third sectors, the need for all charities, but especially smaller ones, to become more "commercially savvy" has never been greater. Traditional sources of funding are drying up for many charities and greater commercial and entrepreneurial acumen is needed if they are to continue to maintain the services they provide to their community. Indeed, for many charities, their very survival is now at stake.

The danger could be that workers in the third sector are predominantly motivated by the cause their charity supports and see "being commercial" as a distraction from their primary goal. Whilst this is totally understandable and, in many ways entirely laudable, the harsh reality is that commerciality is key for all organisations, regardless of sector, shape, size and core purpose.

In recognition of this challenge, the third sector is increasingly seeking to attract these commercial skills from the private sector and also raise the standards of corporate governance, which can often be much weaker in the third sector. Senior business leaders are now often being targeted for leadership roles in the third sector and it can be a very worthwhile and rewarding exercise for both parties. However, success cannot be guaranteed. A senior leader from the private sector needs to understand how the third sector operates and must allow for the inevitable unique challenges that are presented. For example, in my own charity, Action for M.E. at least 50% of the trustees have the illness and it is not reasonable, or indeed fair, to expect the same level of personal energy to be expended by the trustees on lengthy board meetings as may often be the case in the private sector. However, this difficulty can easily be overcome by building in rest-breaks during meetings and ensuring that board time is devoted only to the most important issues. Extensive use of sub committees and conference calls to help minimise travel are techniques that can also help. It is also important for such newcomers to be able to identify strongly with the cause that the charity supports, perhaps due to some particular personal insight or connection. In the world of M.E. there is much understandable anger at the lack of progress in achieving recognition of the illness and also the development of effective treatments, or indeed a cure. This often results in unfair criticism being directed at those researching the illness and also the charities involved. It is important not to hit back, but to be able to understand those criticisms and then use them as motivation to re-double one's efforts on behalf of those people.

Going forward, strong collaboration and effective partnerships between the third sector and the private sector are really crucial, both from a skills transfer perspective and also from a fundraising perspective.

In this extremely useful book, Kay and Tanja show how to get the most from a charity-corporate relationship by setting out a really clear Ten-Point Action Plan for sustained success. I commend it to you.

Alan Cook, CBE

Corporates are from Mars... chose **Action for M.E.** as its charity partner because of their ambitious and innovative approach to achieving their mission: to transform the world of M.E.

M.E. is a chronic, fluctuating illness affecting 250,000 men, women and children in the UK. It may be diagnosed as Chronic Fatigue Syndrome (CFS) or Post-Viral Fatigue Syndrome (PVFS). Symptoms vary but can include overwhelming exhaustion, persistent muscle and/or joint pain, sleep disturbance, memory and concentration problems.

The National Institute for Health and Clinical Excellence says these symptoms can be as disabling as multiple sclerosis, lupus, rheumatoid arthritis or congestive heart failure – yet people with M.E. still encounter scepticism and ignorance. Despite the prevalence of the illness there is as yet no diagnostic test or cure.

Action for M.E. works tirelessly to provide information and support, while campaigning for better services, more effective treatments and greater investment in research – until its vision is finally achieved and M.E. is overcome.

Donate at: www.actionforme.org.uk

ACKNOWLEDGEMENTS

Funding was generously given from enlightened and passionate corporate partners to help bring this book to life as a free best-practice guide. Our sponsors see the benefits of this guide not only for themselves, but for the charity sector as a whole, which will benefit from a more structured approach to getting the best from its own partnerships.

Our thanks also go to an amazing set of individuals who freely gave time in their busy schedules to provide their own unique insights into the corporate-charity relationship.

With thanks to family and friends for their encouragement to transform an idea into reality. Glynis Allen and Kenneth Rothwell for being such passionate guardians of the apostrophe, to Jan Madden for the final edit, and Tanja Rasmussen, for being such a good sounding board, endless re-reading and helping with the research.

To Simon and Jonathan at CST The Gate for giving the confidence and the ability to publish. And thanks to Sally and a holiday in Valencia for getting me started.

Our thanks go to:

Argos
Deloitte
Excell Group Ltd
Fujitsu UK & Ireland
G4S
Linklaters
Morrisons
Nomura
Reckitt Benckiser
Royal Mail Group
Sainsbury's
Tesco

Bromley by Bow Centre
Camfed
Help for Heroes
Help the Hospices
Save the Children
Teenage Cancer Trust
The Myton Hospices
Whizz-Kidz

Our experts:
Alan Cook, CBE

Mark Astarita
Gavin Bounds
Douglas Campbell-Rouse
Simon Davies
Johnathan Evans
Lord Howard
Stephen Howard
Thomas Hughes-Hallett
Martin Johnston
Steve Moore
Campbell Robb
Caroline Waters, OBE

CONTENTS

INTRODUCTION

Approximately £1.4 billion finds its way to the charity sector from around 100 of the UK's largest businesses.[1]

The question is: can more funding be leveraged from the corporate sector to support the third sector?

Corporate-charity partnerships have been around for a long time. Collaborative models can be a great success. Many charities who are experienced in working with business see their brand profile and revenues dramatically increase as a result of a corporate relationship. Equally, there are examples of frustration and disappointment when the partnership fails to deliver against expectations. Indeed, some partnerships have proven costly to the charity. Even the selection process can be arduous, some charities argue they cannot win an open staff-selection process, believing size or attractiveness is a barrier, whilst others know that the power of their brand appeal will secure a win on most attempts.

The partnership model is just one option in the arsenal of ideas that the charity has to enable it to meet its needs; equally, it is only part of the process that a corporate will use to deploy its corporate responsibility strategy. Current economic challenges are placing financial pressures on the third sector and, as the vision for "The Big Society" takes shape, more will be expected from relationships that draw on expertise from the private sector to help deliver creative solutions to third-sector organisations.

The challenge to business is how to create sustainable and more impactful relationships with the charity sector. Successful partnerships with a charity should be regarded as a strategic issue and a key component in the development of an organisation's brand values, people engagement strategy and ultimately its way of doing business.

The challenge to charities is to think more broadly and more strategically. Charities that are innovative in how they approach the value and benefits of a partnership stand to gain more. Understanding the wider potential that a business partner can deliver will help the charity take full advantage of the expertise and support that a business has to offer. Fundraising is of course part of this story – a good partnership, however, can add greater value to both partners.

Charities and corporates will have different value sets and different expectations as well as different ways of approaching a partnership. John Gray, in his famous book, "Men are from Mars, Women are from Venus", helps men and women to remember their differences in order to find a harmonious relationship.

This guide reminds us that good intentions are not enough; a successful charity-corporate partnership requires planning and hard work from both partners.

The purpose of this guide is to offer a more systematic approach for managing corporate-charity partnerships.

Our premise is that concentrating on the process is the best way to achieve a successful partnership.

Through the stories of successful partnerships and the insights of some amazing individuals, the guide provides advice to both charities and corporates on how to realise greater benefits and deliver more meaningful activities from partnership work.

[1] London Benchmarking Group Annual Review 2010

THE TEN-POINT ACTION PLAN

Using the analogy of a marriage, we have developed a Ten-Point Action Plan, which we work through chapter by chapter, for managing a charity-corporate partnership.

Action Point 1: Single (chapter 1) – Explores the importance of pre-planning and establishing a clear purpose for wanting to engage in such a partnership.

Action Point 2: Dating (chapter 2) – Looks at how to set out a compelling proposal for a partnership. Both partners need to think through what they can give and not just what they want to receive.

Action Point 3: Engaged (chapter 3) – Examines the preparation time needed once a partnership has been agreed. Getting to know each other is vital for honest communication and joint working.

Action Point 4: Vows (chapter 4) – Looks at the importance of the formal agreement. The use of a Memorandum of Understanding can help set the boundaries for working and ensure problems can be dealt with professionally.

Action Point 5: Honeymoon (chapter 5) – The first stages of any relationship are important. Leadership is without doubt a key ingredient to success. Getting all the "in-laws" together to agree to give their support adds momentum and gets the partnership off to a flying start.

Action Point 6: Marriage (chapter 6) – Explores the importance of stakeholder engagement and managing the ups and downs of a partnership.

Action Point 7: Benefits (chapter 7) – An essential part of any marriage is reciprocity. It is important to understand how to deliver value creation for both partners.

Action Point 8: Date nights (chapter 8) – Examines the importance of allowing a partnership to discover new ways of sustaining progress and looks at the value of recognition and celebrating success.

Action Point 9: Beyond marriage (chapter 9) – The time allocated to a partnership passes all too quickly. Effective legacy planning helps secure a long-lasting connection.

Action Point 10: Reflections (chapter 10) – Taking the time to reflect on a partnership helps identify key moments of success and lessons learned.

We hope you will find inspiration from the case studies and that their success helps you and your partnership.

CHAPTER ONE

Single

ARE YOU A CHARITY – LOOKING TO GET HITCHED?

ARE YOU A CORPORATE – LOOKING TO SHARE THE LOVE?

The reasons for forming a charity-corporate partnership for social good are varied. For the corporate, a history of philanthropy and tradition might be the only rationale for seeking a charity partner. A more likely reason will be a sophisticated approach to consumer engagement, or there might be a specific business need for an important stakeholder relationship. Employee engagement is often a key success indicator expected by the corporate.

For the charity, expected outcomes can be equally diverse – driven by the need to raise brand profile or a more pressing commercial imperative to raise funds. A charity relationship can also be an important lever for influencing behaviour of a corporate. Such a partnership can provide a wealth of expertise, volunteers, assets and facilities, it can also help reduce operational costs, drive efficiency and improve the skill base of a charity.

Whatever the reason for seeking a collaborative commitment for good, there is an important first step through which both corporate and charity alike must work whilst they are single. Both charity and corporate must be clear on what they are looking for in a partnership.

"The purpose behind our Charity of the Year is to inspire and motivate staff and customers to get behind a cause that makes a real difference. We know this improves customers' experience of Tesco and engages our colleagues."

Ruth Girardet,
CR and Communities Director. Tesco

"Knowing what you are trying to achieve helps you to be clear about your goals, you have to have a sense of purpose which underpins your proposition in order to make it meaningful when asking a corporate partner to help you."

Ruth Owen,
CEO. Whizz-Kidz

FINDINGS:

Single – Why partnerships are sought

The reasons for wanting to set up a charity-corporate partnership may be triggered by different needs:

Win/win: What emerged from talking to corporate responsibility (CR)[2] professionals is that the corporate has become more sophisticated and demanding in its expectations of charity partnerships. From the corporate perspective, there is a strong expectation that any partnership has to be a two-way street.

This search for a win/win is gaining momentum and what is clear from the evidence looked at here is that the win for the corporate is no longer just about a good PR headline, but tangible bottom-line benefits.

This approach can of course place huge demands on a charity who may be asked to deliver a project outside their core objectives or simply be overwhelmed when a large corporate suddenly gives a massive boost to revenue. It also raises the whole issue about how to measure success in this area. Some charities may argue that corporates are becoming too demanding.

The trick is to get the balance right. The research for this guide clearly indicates that the corporate purpose for seeking a charity partnership is becoming much more strategic and aligned to business objectives. The more experienced charities understand the wider potential gain of a partnership with many seeking to grow this source of revenue.

Access to expertise: Many third-sector organisations are recognising the benefits of engaging pro bono expertise to help drive efficiency and cost savings. Corporates are a rich source of talent and a partnership helps generate innovative sharing of expertise and access to volunteers.

Raise awareness: A charity may wish to access a corporate's large network of stakeholders from customers to suppliers in order to share information on a campaign issue and thus raise the profile of the charity. Equally, a corporate may wish to further its brand reputation.

New revenue streams: Partnerships are capable of realising large sources of new revenue. Mobilising consumer engagement is often a critical driver for both corporate and charity alike.

Employee engagement: Recruiting and retaining talent is a significant business driver. More and more people are now expecting to work for a corporate that has a strong ethical approach and that enables employees to get involved in social causes. Proud employees are passionate advocates and employers are looking for effective ways to secure loyalty.

Respected brands: Businesses are becoming more attuned to developing sustainable and impactful relationships with the third sector. Successful partnerships are regarded as a central component in the development of the organisation's values and brand, of its engagement strategy and ultimately its commercial success. The rise of professionalism for CR in the corporate world came across strongly in all the case studies we looked at and a phrase that was used by several contributors was that "CR was a core strategic issue for their business".

[2] Job titles varied for this position – this book uses the term CR professional to cover a range of titles.

Starbucks is all about backing young people. All of the charity partnership work provides volunteering and development opportunities for colleagues. The five-year partnership with the National Literacy Trust is focused on the National Young Readers programme. Disadvantaged children are encouraged to visit libraries and discover reading for enjoyment. The partnership will generate over £1 million in addition to raising awareness around literacy.

Customer expectations: The recent financial crisis has magnified customer expectations that corporates should give back to society from where they draw their profits.

Recognition: With a new business emphasis on CR, the demand for recognition is also on the increase. The past 30 years of Business in the Community has created an impressive portfolio of corporate achievement: prestigious awards, leading national standards such as the CommunityMark, a sought-after CR Index and the attention of 850 CEOs who are members of BITC. The FTSE4Good index is tracking behaviour offering ethical investment and the standard annual report is starting to integrate CR as a key business measure of success.

Wider purpose: New partnership models and a wider range of benefits are emerging. This opens up the market to those charities who in the past may have found winning a traditional "Charity of the Year" difficult due to their core brand proposition being less attractive. Corporates appear to be much more open to the courtship process.

Conclusion: There are many reasons why both corporate and charity will seek out a partnership. What we can say with certainty is that the days of a corporate being satisfied with just handing over a cheque to a charity at the end of the year are long gone for many CR directors. "Partnerships are now expected to deliver a far more dramatic impact than just financial support."[3] Charities are responding to this change with innovative solutions that seek to satisfy all the drivers for wanting a partnership.

[3] Deloitte, Emerging Partnership Models between Business and the Third Sector (2010).

CASE HISTORY

Whizz-Kidz on being single

Whizz-Kidz had a core strategic goal to reduce the waiting time for getting a wheelchair to a child: "A Child – A Chair – A Day".

In 2005 there were 391 children waiting for wheelchairs and Whizz-Kidz wanted to remove this waiting list. The cost would be £1.5 million.

Money would clearly help to solve this problem, funding the wheelchair for each child that was waiting. However, money alone would not tackle fundamental supply-chain problems with the NHS or the expertise of the charity itself in lobbying for change.

The existing supply chain for children's wheelchairs was cumbersome, slow and expensive. Whizz-Kidz needed to get to grips with the thorny issue of procurement and take on a massive challenge of raising the money to fund the wheelchairs.

Whizz-Kidz knew exactly what they were looking for in that perfect match. Their purpose was to:

- Find expertise on supply-chain management and a company not afraid to take on the challenge.
- Establish themselves as a change agent able to lobby Government to challenge the system that had created the unacceptable standards in the first place. Whizz-Kidz wanted a partner that would help them achieve this change.
- Raise their profile and become known nationally to help generate a more sustainable income stream. Whizz-Kidz was a relatively small charity in 2005, but they had big aspirations.
- Establish the foundations for the future growth of the charity and attract more volunteers.

Whizz-Kidz had a purpose in mind that went beyond fundraising, seeking value in expertise which would strengthen the charity's position.

TOP TIP: "Know your purpose each time you are looking for a partnership. Set out a compelling goal that makes a real difference to people's lives, something that will really resonate with the corporate you are trying to impress."
Ruth Owen, CEO. Whizz-Kidz

CASE HISTORY

Tesco on being single

A key objective for Tesco is to support local communities and be a good neighbour. This is an issue customers care deeply about; it is also the way Tesco believes is right to do business. The annual Charity of the Year Partnership enables Tesco to support communities across the UK and provides a variety of opportunities for customers to get involved and make a difference themselves. Fundraising activities in-store help create a warm and friendly atmosphere, making customers feel closer to staff and positive about shopping in Tesco.

In making a decision about whom to chose, the CR team are looking for a proposition that has a clear objective that colleagues and customers can get behind. A clear objective helps communicate progress and inspire people to get involved.

The Whizz-Kidz proposition was extremely compelling and they were selected on the strength of their campaign and potential for Tesco to make a real and lasting difference to the lives of young people with mobility impairments as well as to the fabric and nature of the charity itself.

At the beginning of the partnership Tesco and Whizz-Kidz set clear objectives to engage the public in funding 391 wheelchairs and to increase brand awareness for Whizz-Kidz. Whizz-Kidz developed such a comprehensive approach to working right across Tesco that it opened up previously untapped income streams from the Distribution Division of 25,000 employees which alone raised a phenomenal £620,000. The total raised was £3.4 million, helping over 750 children.

The wider benefits came from employee engagement, including tapping into the expertise at Tesco to help strengthen the working practices at Whizz-Kidz, access to Tesco expertise in procurement to tackle the poor supply of wheelchairs and access to large audiences who became volunteers for Whizz-Kidz.

The incredible success with Whizz-Kidz was the result of a simple, tangible, emotive proposition that had a clear goal.

TOP TIP:"A corporate will have thought through exactly why it wants a Charity of the Year and exactly what it expects to achieve. The language of goals and achievement will be embedded into their thought process. A charity should be able to reflect this when setting out its own purpose and what it can offer a corporate partner."

Ruth Girardet, CR and Communities Director. Tesco

ACTION POINT 1:

Be clear on what you are seeking from a partnership before you enter into negotiations. Set out what benefits you desire and what you can offer in return. Whatever the motivation, size, expertise or field of work, Action Point 1 is the same for both charity and corporate – you must know what you want.

Macmillan Cancer Support and Boots had a clear purpose to give the two million people in the UK currently living with cancer, and their family and friends, the information and support they need. Their partnership aims to do this by bringing information about living with cancer to the UK's local high streets, regional communities, and on line.

Single – Know your purpose

As we have seen, a charity-corporate partnership can have a number of purposes.

Draw up a partnership purpose paper. This must set out what you are prepared to compromise on and what you can offer. And indeed what you can handle if all your dreams come true! This purpose paper acts as a cornerstone for all your other decisions; it sets the tone for your pitch and guides your expectations. This is not the same as knowing the charity or company vision and the core organisational goals. Set out a clear purpose for each different partnership.

Identify measurable objectives and quantify what success could look like: such as how many volunteers you need, or what kind of expertise you are looking for. Be clear on what you are looking for and why.

Identify the type of partner you would like to work with and draw up a potential target list. By having a strong sense of your own purpose you will be better placed to agree a shared sense of purpose and joint strategy (see chapter 3). A clear purpose gives you a reference point against which to review progress and measure the success of your overall partnership strategy.

Think through what you cannot do. The very nature of the third sector means that ethics and standards are core to the organisation, but they are especially important for the charity-corporate partnership, both because of the need to balance objectives of the charity and because of the public nature of these relationships. A charity needs to have a risk-analysis process for ensuring it has researched any potential partner and that it has an exit strategy should an ethical dilemma emerge once a partnership has started. Imagine a children's charity finding themselves with a lucrative relationship with a retailer only to discover a challenge to human rights hidden in a supply chain. Unforeseen problems will occur, what is important is that you have a process for dealing with the ethical question.

A charity partnership can also be a powerful agent for change and sometimes choosing a partner that seems a strange bedfellow and somewhat at odds with your mission can bring about the greatest internal change. For example – an environmental charity working with an oil company or an equality charity supporting a corporate that has had a discrimination issue can lead to important changes. As long as clear parameters are set and the ethical boundaries are made clear a partnership is possible.

SECRETS TO SUCCESS

Single charity? – finding the perfect corporate partner

Good intentions are not enough – make sure you know what you are looking for.

Exercise:

What's your brand proposition? A charity's name is a valuable asset and each charity should be clear what its brand proposition is. Before forming a charity partnership, the charity must have thought through what value their name and brand offer. Many corporates will want a proposition based on "cause-related marketing".[4] How will your stakeholders respond to seeing the charity brand aligned with a corporate brand?

What do you expect to gain? There are many reasons why a relationship with a commercial partner may be sought; make sure you know what you expect to gain. A partnership might not be based on a direct financial proposition but could be based on access to expert advice or linking synergies between both brands for a direct consumer appeal.

What can you give? The days of a corporate just handing across a cheque are over. This will be a partnership and they will want a lot in return. What can you offer in terms of employee and consumer engagement, expertise and brand profile? Cash, although important, will only be one of many benefits; a corporate will also want volunteering opportunities or the chance to make a measurable difference. You will need to know your boundaries so you can say *no* to a corporate request if that request will place too much pressure on your core activities. Volunteering opportunities may not be possible. It's important to be honest in this respect.

[4] Sue Adkins Cause Related Marketing: Who Cares Wins (Butterworth-Heinemann, 1999).

What is your ethical policy? Charities must be able to articulate their ethical stance so that any future partner can understand which areas can be compromised and which cannot. This approach is vital, especially if a charity wishes to operate as a lever for change to help improve a corporate's behaviour. A charity may have to decide if a commercial relationship is in the best interest of the charity.

Do you have enough resource? Any partnership will demand attention. Do you have sufficient resources to carry out a risk assessment? How are you going to manage any future partnership? How far will you go to please your new partner? How will you monitor progress? What happens if you become overwhelmed by a big corporate partner?

Have you got access to expert advice? The management of any charity partnership must adhere to tax and charity legislation. The charity may well have knowledge of the Charities Act 2006 and various regulations but don't assume any new corporate partner will have such knowledge. You will need to remain vigilant and in control of any agreement.

How are the charity board of trustees kept informed? Ultimately it will be the board of trustees that will have to deal with any challenges resulting from a corporate partnership. How will you keep the board informed?

Coach your teams and explore all the issues that impact on why you want a corporate partner, this will ensure you really know your purpose.

SECRETS TO SUCCESS

Single corporate? – finding a great charity partner

Planning and goal setting are part of the everyday language for corporate organisations – Preparing for a charity partnership is no different.

Exercise:

Why do you want a charity partnership? A corporate should have a clear understanding of what it hopes to achieve by having an association with a charity.

What is your primary driver?

How does this fit into your overall CR approach? Do you have a wider CR strategy covering a much wider subject matter and if so how are you going to balance all your objectives with the desire to have a successful focus on the charity?

What do you want to gain? Are you clear where the emphasis lies? Is employee engagement or consumer engagement your priority? What can you give a charity and what do you want back? This is an important debate to have as it will have an impact on the size and type of charity you want to partner with. Do you want to "own" a subject and make a massive difference? Will you have multiple strategic partners working on a theme? These are all questions that will impact on how you manage your partnership.

How long will the partnership last? A lot of thought must be given to this question. How fast can your communications take effect? What are you trying to achieve? For Royal Mail and Barnardos, employing young people and developing mentoring programmes was a key objective, this was clearly going to be a long-term project so a three-year time scale was agreed. Tesco are extremely efficient at their communications so changing a partner each year is now part of their CR approach.

How will you identify your charity partner? Does a theme matter? Do you want to align a charity to a core-business objective such as the environment, skills, youth, older people, digital exclusion or do you want to go with the views of your employees? Is your core objective employee engagement or is it about using your expertise to enhance a charity's ability to deliver?

Are there any potential risks? Think through the ethics question for a charity. Are there any potential risk areas in your business? Are you confident of your supply-chain practices for example? What assurances can you give a charity?

How will you choose a partner? By knowing your purpose, you will recognise the best way to choose your charity partner. Remember, a perfect partner might be out there, but one who would never put themselves forward for a charity partnership if a staff vote was a deciding factor. How can you help those charities who might not attract the majority staff vote?

Working through the above exercise will help you to understand what to expect from a partner and what you can give.

GAVIN BOUNDS

Fujitsu Chief Operating Officer, shares his business perspective

"Fujitsu is in the process of scoping out a new approach to CR within its UK and Ireland business, which will take centre stage within our growth strategy. The intention is to seek out a charity partnership that will start in April 2012 and last for a minimum of two years. Although we have engaged with charities in the past this will be the first time we will have formalised such a relationship. We have created a CR Board and it is really important that the executive team understands exactly what a partnership can deliver in a win/win scenario. For Fujitsu our purpose for wanting a strategic partnership with a charity can be broadly summarised as:

Leadership: To enable the new leadership team to set the tone and direction as an employer who believes in responsible business practice and who cares about employee well-being, the community and the environment. To help demonstrate that the new leadership team will deliver on its vision and proposals and that it will listen to, and act upon, colleague opinion.

Employee engagement: To help influence and enhance our employee engagement strategy. The charity partnership will be used as a focal point for team building and growing the sense of pride we feel in working for Fujitsu. Key measures have been identified to track success within our employee engagement.

Communication: To deliver an inspiring and engaging communication tool for colleagues and external stakeholders that will enhance the corporate story, helping to build a respected brand and position Fujitsu as a responsible employer.

Supplier engagement: To provide a link to suppliers and a route to supplier engagement.

Personal development: A charity partner will be sought that can offer the opportunity for personal colleague development, for example, project management/sharing of expertise/team leadership etc.

Impact on society: Of course the partnership must deliver demonstrable impact. Clear success indicators must be set to enable the partnership to celebrate achievements building the communication and engagement story. The partnership will be looking for a core purpose that can be focused on to deliver change that benefits people's lives. Where possible, a unique proposition will be developed.

To raise funds: Any charity partner will expect their revenue stream to increase as a result of the partnership. A partnership takes a great deal of effort and resource to deliver. An expectation must be set, with the company being prepared to underwrite some of this expectation.

Efficiency/expertise: In addition to fundraising the company will also be seeking a charity partner that can benefit from Fujitsu being a technology partner on a specific project."

TOP TIP: "By being clear on our purpose we hope to make it easier for a charity to set out a proposal to us. Having the 'right-fit' strategic partner will allow us to make a difference to people's lives, our employees, our suppliers, our customers and wider society."

MARK ASTARITA

Chair of the Institute of Fundraising and CEO of the Red Cross offers his charity perspective

"Charity-corporate partnerships are fantastic – they can be so positive for both parties and be worth so much more than just hard cash. The trick is that charities must be business savvy to unlock the value that a good partnership can offer.

I believe charities often underestimate the power and value of their brand. There are a lot of 'cuddly' causes out there, but pitched correctly, you can make the right offer and compete for that lucrative partnership. It is important to get your proposition right and know what you are seeking to achieve.

Charities can offer a lot to lift a corporate brand, a positive association can often soften a corporate approach and help change public perception. You need to be really confident before you agree to any partnership that you are 100% sure of any brand association. This can be a double edged sword, a delicate balance between securing funding and being associated with, for example, poor employment practices or human rights failures in a complex supply chain.

What charities must do is to involve all parts of the organisation, it's not just about the fundraising team! You have to think about how you can add real depth to any relationship.

For example, at Red Cross we work with Land Rover. They train our drivers with advance driving skills and we train their colleagues in first aid. By always thinking through the win/win scenarios you can really embed the relationship right across both organisations.

Successful partnerships are all about relationships. To maximise these partnerships, senior management from both organisations MUST be engaged and 'in the room' – you need to show that the relationship is important top down."

TOP TIP: "The corporate sector exists to make a profit. Charities need to demonstrate that they can understand this and really deliver a professional corporate service."

SUMMARY

Single with a purpose

Knowing your purpose helps to map out your objectives, balance the ethical questions, stay true to your purpose and establish a strong reference point against which to measure success.

A purpose statement will have:

- Expectation of what a partner could offer
- What can be offered (and what cannot)
- What type of partner is sought
- Clarity of ethics/boundaries
- An understanding of the value of the brand

A charity might need access to:

- Expertise
- Volunteers
- New revenue sources
- Equipment/buildings
- Resources

A corporate might want to achieve:

- Employment engagement
- Personal development
- Brand reputation
- Customer engagement
- Cause-related marketing

TEN-POINT ACTION PLAN		
Action Point 1	Single	Know your purpose ✓

CHAPTER TWO

Dating

ARE YOU A CHARITY – NERVOUSLY ABOUT TO PROPOSE?

ARE YOU ARE CORPORATE – ANXIOUS ABOUT SAYING YES?

Once you know your purpose and are ready to start dating, how you craft your proposal is mission critical. You need to create a compelling proposition with which your potential partner will identify.

For the corporate, issuing a clear brief of what you expect will help the charity match your expectations. It is important to explain how the decision for choosing a partner is to be made, as this will help the charity to tailor its messages to the deciding audience.

For the charity, any proposition put forward should have a sense of true partnership. There needs to be a bold statement of what is being offered as well as what is expected in return. A simple headline "wow" factor highlighting the difference that can be made together. Researching your potential partner will help you get the tone of your seduction just right.

Whatever you are hoping to achieve from your partnership – the second step is the same for everyone in the dating game. You need a compelling proposal.

"I am looking for something new and different to help keep colleagues engaged. You can't just do the same thing each year with different partners – we need fresh new approaches that are innovative and make a difference."

Kerry Buckley,
Buying Assistant. Sainsbury's

"There is no right template that you just follow, it is all about hitting the synergies. It's not about being a worthy cause and expecting people to help. Your proposal has to be tailored to meet the expectations of the corporate partner."

Ruth Freeman,
Director of Income Generation and Marketing. The Myton Hospices

FINDINGS:

Dating – what makes a compelling proposal

There is no one perfect proposal – they are simply different, with different objectives

Usually, it is the corporate who determines the opportunity for a partnership and it is the charity that has to convince the corporate they are the perfect match. This process can be very competitive and developing a compelling proposal is vital. There is a rise in the courtship process (as opposed to the competitive pitch). More and more charities are seeking out corporate partnerships with innovative ideas for collaboration. As companies become more experienced in managing these types of partnership they are increasingly more confident in tackling difficult subjects.

Style of presentations: The presentation style will be influenced by the decision-making process. If the decision is being made by a management panel then the proposition must be compelling and well thought through and play to the corporate CR strategy. If the decision is being made purely by a staff vote then the presentation will need to be equally compelling but with a different emphasis and tone. The impact, when pitching to staff, needs to be more about helping people together – the power of collective action.

Range of selection methods: Companies use a range of methods, from a vote totally controlled by colleagues to a colleague-nomination process with a management decision to a pure management choice. Examples:

• **Sainsbury's** main purpose was to seek local engagement to help drive local knowledge. Colleagues nominated potential partners. A panel of senior managers then made a choice from the top four nominated charities.

• **Royal Mail Group** identified staff engagement as a key purpose. That purpose helped define the staff vote. Staff voted for a theme and against this theme a mapping exercise discovered the charities which best matched the core objectives. A panel of senior managers then selected three charities that could all meet these objectives. The final three charities were subject to an open staff vote.

• **Tesco** has been running its Charity of the Year since 1987 and has raised over £60 million for a wide variety of UK charitable causes. Every year Tesco welcomes applications from charities which operate across the UK and in local communities close to its stores. The decision is made by a panel of Tesco colleagues.

• **Fujitsu** has crafted an approach which involves asking charities to complete a simple expression of interest form. Colleagues can also put forward suggestions. The CR team will analyse these and present a long list of nominations to the CR Board who will decide on three charities to go forward for a staff vote.

A meaningful proposition: If a charity is seeking out a corporate partner then they need to be creative in how they make that approach. CR professionals revealed a sense of frustration when discussing how they received requests from charities. The generic (in some cases photocopied) letters arriving in the post will almost certainly elicit a standard "no thank you" response. Requests that showed little appreciation of the corporates CR approach were also frustrating when a little research would no doubt have revealed what the corporate was trying to achieve. On average, a corporate can receive upwards of 30 such requests each week.

Between July and August 2010, staff and members at The Co-operative cast over 42,000 votes to elect Mencap the Co-operative 'Charity of the Year'. The money raised will help launch a new project called "Inspire Me", which aims to support 20,000 young people with a learning disability. The fundraising target is £5 million.

The Myton Hospices have carried out research with decision makers in smaller companies locally to try and understand their motivations and in 100% of cases they say that charitable support is decided in one way or another by their staff. Larger corporates tend to involve a panel in the final decision, unless the choice is pushed down to local level as with Sainsbury's and Waitrose in which cases staff are much more influential.

Choose your partner deliberately: A compelling proposal can result from matching the needs of two organisations. This might not be a traditional Charity of the Year but an agreement to work collaboratively for a common aim. Usually these imaginative partnerships result from a process of courtship.

Multiple partners are common: Corporates often work with more than one partner to tackle a particular issue.

Barclaycard Horizons is a unique partnership with Family Action, Gingerbread and Citizens Advice. This project brings together three expert partners to support one-parent families. Over 270,000 families have been helped with a combination of support, money advice, grants towards education and training and help with returning to work.

"As Head of Social Action for Royal Mail Group, I received an email from Ruth Owen that was only a few lines long. The purpose of Whizz-Kidz was simple: to engage Royal Mail's expertise to help deliver a mail campaign at no cost to Whizz-Kidz. Ruth did her homework and researched the right person to approach with a simple but compelling ask.

> Dear Kay
> I recently sat next to one of your Non-Executive Directors, Baroness Prosser, who said you had done brilliant things at Royal Mail. She suggested you may be able to give me some advice on mail logistics to help us deliver a project with Tesco and the Blue Peter Appeal. If you have time may I buy you a coffee and talk you through what we need to achieve.
> Ruth Owen
> CEO Whizz-Kidz

Such a simple, clever email: she mentioned she had met a non-executive director of Royal Mail (leadership reference, I was not going to ignore a NED) who had suggested she contact me as I was brilliant (charmed me!) for some advice (advice is free) on logistics (that's what Royal Mail does) for a charity venture with Tesco (who are an important customer to Royal Mail). Could she buy me a coffee? This ask was easy to say yes to, I involved the Royal Mail key account director for Tesco who jumped at the chance to help his customer, the result being we helped deliver a great project. As a result, Ruth was able to cultivate a relationship with a new corporate. Not a Charity of the Year status – but none the less a good relationship. Ruth Owen had a clear purpose. She knew the value of her proposition to Royal Mail, she knew Tesco would be a key driver in securing our engagement and as such created a clever three-way partnership."

Size doesn't necessarily matter: The economy of these partnerships is changing and new models are emerging (see chapter 7). Some corporates have made a move to local choice where they operate multiple sites across the UK as the corporate seeks to improve its local knowledge and local impact; this model is mostly seen in retail. The larger corporates, especially in banking and services, are still favouring one overarching charity. Many corporates have multiple partners challenging different issues.

The Carphone Warehouse has always had a core proposition based on connecting people. They chose a smaller charity partner called Get Connected, whose purpose is to ensure that every young person in the UK can connect with the support they need. A perfect match.

Launched in 2008, Waitrose's Community Matters initiative donated over £2.7 million to 8,500 local projects in 2010/11. Using tokens provided at the till, customers decide how much of the £1,000 monthly total is given to three local charities. This process helps to raise local awareness as well as money.

Conclusion: What is clear is the third sector now has much more choice in how they pitch for a partnership. Corporates are seeking innovative solutions and have the capacity to work strategically with a charity for a specific purpose. Charities can be much more bold in offering a compelling proposal and make a direct approach and work though a "courtship" process. The more competitive style selection will require an innovative pitch that sets out a clear win/win scenario with imaginative requests that are not just about the cheque presentation. The request should aim to hit a number of key measures that a corporate is seeking to influence, not least its brand reputation.

CASE HISTORY

The Myton Hospices on dating

TOP TIP: "Treat every pitch as unique. Start with a blank piece of paper. Everyone wants to feel extra special during that all important courtship, don't take anything for granted."
Ruth Freeman, Director of Income Generation and Marketing. The Myton Hospices

The Myton Hospices is a relatively small charity based in Warwick, Rugby and Coventry. Standing out from the crowd is important when preparing a pitch as often the competition is against bigger charities as well as some popular local ones. Each potential partner is different, so when preparing for a pitch, sticking to a template is risky. It is better to approach each one with a clean sheet of paper.

The proposal needs to look for synergies and identify on what levels the two partners could interact. What makes you interesting? Are there any aspects of your work that has links to their business, e.g. retail, communications, logistics, technology, because companies like to use their expertise as well as their money. It is important to know the corporate style and what they are likely to find attractive in a proposal. It is also useful to weigh up the competition to find out what it is that you can offer that they can't!

When preparing a proposal don't just research the corporate in isolation: think about their customers and their suppliers. Are there any connections between the two organisations already? Research any previous charity partnership, what worked well and what didn't. Make contact with any previous partners and ask for their advice.

CASE HISTORY

Sainsbury's on dating

TOP TIP: "Corporates are looking for a well-thought-through challenge that they can really get behind and it has to be so much more than just a cheque presentation at the end of the year."
Kerry Buckley, Buying Assistant. Sainsbury's

Sainsbury's takes a local approach, allowing each store and centre to get behind a cause that is really important to them. The cause has to be something that colleagues are passionate about. Colleagues nominate local causes from which a short list is selected. The top nominations then come along to present to a panel.

When The Myton Hospices responded to Sainbury's call to action for a new charity partnership there was strong competition from well-known local charities. The proposal focused on how Sainsbury's could add real value to the charity. A series of financial and non-financial goals were offered. The proposal asked for expertise and support.

The Myton Hospices best understood how Sainsbury's could mutually help each organisation's objectives. The presentation was professional and explained in enough detail how the charity operation could match Sainsbury's values and on what the money raised would be spent.

What really stood out was the request for expertise in helping to run the charity retail shops more efficiently.

CASE HISTORY

The Myton Hospices and the BBC local radio

TOP TIP: "You need to develop a proposition that gets you noticed. The tone of your pitch needs to reflect the audience who are making the decision – there is no one size fits all."

Ruth Freeman, Director of Income Generation and Marketing. The Myton Hospices

The pitch made by The Myton Hospices to BBC local radio was very different from that made to Sainsbury's. This particular pitch was very competitive as similar campaigns in the past had raised in excess of £1 million. Particular attention was given to finding a unique angle that would meet the brief set by the BBC. The BBC wanted a fundraising campaign that would inspire their listeners and they also wanted some non-financial goals.

The proposal matched attracting new listeners to the BBC with the opportunity to raise awareness of hospice care.

The pitch focused on four main themes:

- The political debate on end-of-life care and involving listeners in that debate
- The promotion of hospice care, dispelling any myths and removing fear
- The size and demographic of our local donor base – as potential listeners
- The powerful impact of our stories

To make the pitch incredibly powerful, a nurse and a child from the bereavement service gave a first-hand account of the impact of the services at The Myton Hospices.

A radio campaign was developed that promoted dignity and respect in managing the end-of-life process. The campaign was based on raising awareness of this important issue, promoting care for terminally ill people and making sure people in the local community knew that help was available.

The proposal was not based directly on financial impact, but the results would deliver huge cost benefits.

ACTION POINT 2:

The invitation from the corporate and the application from the charity should set out to recognise the benefits to both partners. There is no magic formula for the perfect proposal but each new proposal should aim to match the core objectives of both organisations.

Dating – Create a compelling proposal

The corporate must set out a clear brief of what is expected from a charity proposal. Be specific on the areas of work. It helps to quantify expectations such as capacity for volunteering, fundraising and access to expertise. Set out what is expected in return – what is the key purpose for seeking a partnership?

Think through how the decision is to be made; this will alter how a charity prepares its presentation. Ensure that all the prospective charities know who their audience is.

All the charities who apply should receive good feedback on how any decision was reached. It is vital to have a transparent process that explains the decision-making process and the reasons for the final choice.

As a charity you only get one chance to present your case as to why you should win a charity partnership. Your pitch has to answer all the questions a corporate might have. It must have that winning formula that a corporate is looking for and you will only achieve this if you set out the win/win aspects of a partnership. Make sure you follow the brief set by the corporate in the selection proposal. Ensure you answer all their points. Set out non-financial targets with a clear understanding of their value.

A corporate will want to make a difference – so set out the difference you can achieve together and build your proposal around deliverables that an organisation will be able to measure. An overarching goal is a good motivating factor for a corporate.

Remember a corporate can only make a decision based on the case you as a charity present to them. They need to make an objective decision, so make sure your proposal is thorough, well researched and match perfect.

Sky chose Global Action Plan (GAP) from 170 applicants to form a three-year partnership. Sky was looking for a proposal that would engage and inspire colleagues and customers to take action on climate change. The proposal from GAP supported Sky's environmental aims and demonstrated how the partnership would contribute towards building Sky's reputation as a trusted business and leader on climate change. The decision was made based on the alignment of the two organisations' core objectives.

SECRETS TO SUCCESS

Charity looking to date? – getting the proposal just right

The style and tone of any pitch will be different depending on the partnership model – Know your audience.

Exercise:

Who are the audience/decision-makers? Think about the audience who will be making the decision and ensure that they have all the information they need to make an informed choice. If your charity brand is less well known, you should not see this as a disadvantage when making a pitch to a panel, but as an opportunity to show your strengths and unique focus. If the pitch is to an open staff vote, you will need to position the proposal differently than if you were presenting to a panel.

What's your "wow" factor? You need a big impact goal. There will be a lot of other things a partnership will achieve, but pull out the one big thing that together you can change.

What are you offering? We have seen how corporates are looking to make a difference and make an impact on the communities in which they work. The corporate will be looking for a journey that they can embark upon with a charity to make a measurable difference. Think about what you can offer as a unique insight for a corporate.

Where's the win/win? Make sure any pitch is set out as a two-way process. The aim should be more than just a cheque. It is expected that the partnership will raise money, but this should not be the primary focus of your proposal. Make it more about impact and added value, looking at cost reduction, pro bono work, fundraising and capacity building.

What research can you do? You need to be able to talk the language of the corporate you are aiming to impress. What's the demographic of their employees, who are their customers and their target market? Everyone likes attention – make sure you can show you have made the effort to know your potential partner.

Can you think outside the box? You may be able to approach a target partner through a supplier, key customer or Non-Executive Director. Barnardo's, for example, were able to connect to Fujitsu through Royal Mail Group. Fujitsu are a large supplier to Post Office Ltd so this relationship was leveraged to build support for Barnardo's, who were RMG's Charity Partner.

How can you help a corporate brand? Profit for profit's sake is no longer a sustainable business model post the financial crisis. How can you help a corporate to become a more respected and trusted brand?

SECRETS TO SUCCESS

Corporate looking to date? – finding the perfect fit

Some charities tackle challenging issues – how will you ensure a fair and equal chance to all charities who are seeking a partnership?

Exercise:

Is there a clear brief for the selection process? A clear brief is vital to help the charity when inviting a pitch. It is against this brief that they will base their proposal. Set out core messages that you want them to address so that each pitch can be compared fairly.

What parameters are you going to set? Are you going to request a certain size of charity, are you looking for a UK-wide approach? The parameters that are set will preclude a lot of charities from applying – are you sure this approach works? How will you ensure you can have due diligence and transparency during the process of selection?

Who will be making the decision? Really think through the mechanics of the selection process. It needs to be open and fair, giving each charity an opportunity to present itself in a favourable light. An open staff vote is a great engagement tool, but what support can you offer to overcome perception barriers? How can you encourage support for more challenging issues and less well known charities?

How will you sell your goals? It is important that you think through any indicator of success. If you set a financial target of £1 million and you raise £900,000, is this success or a missed target? Be careful how you position financial indicators as every penny raised for a charity and every person engaged is a good news story. You want to be able to celebrate the partnership so make sure your goals are achievable. How will you manage expectations – just because a previous charity relationship may have raised £1 million does not guarantee this level of success in the future.

Does the selection process have a cost to charities? Competing in a selection process can be costly. Will you help with this cost? Can you offer guidance to a charity on how to deliver a cost-effective pitch?

Is the process transparent? Make sure your selection process is transparent. Be prepared to give constructive feedback to all the charities who pitched to help their learning for future attempts. Charities were quite critical during this research that feedback from the corporate was often weak.

DOUGLAS CAMPBELL-ROUSE

Corporate Partnerships Director at Save the Children gives his view on the charity-corporate relationship

"In 2010 Save the Children more than doubled corporate donations from £4.5 million to £10.3 million, including gifts in-kind. The ambition is to achieve £30 million.

The charity sector is unbelievably competitive – much tougher than trading in the City and way more enjoyable. It's also much harder work. My experience from running the treasury team at Dresdner Kleinwort Benson has helped me bring a new commercial focus to the charity.

When I arrived at Save the Children I reviewed the operation for corporate fundraising, I proposed a new structure and asked everyone to apply for changed roles. Four were successful and we immediately set about recruiting new staff. A new business team was formed which focused on approaching companies with very clear partnership proposals. Getting a smart ask together is critical. Once a partnership is won, it is handed over to an account management team that looks not only to deliver what's been agreed, but also to grow and stretch and develop the partnership into other areas.

We have focused on utilising the breadth of Save the Children's work to engage with companies in different ways and to look for partners who are well aligned with the charity's work in health education, hunger, prevention and, obviously, with children. We do an awful lot of research and we approach companies with a very tailored partnership opportunity where there are some very clear tangible benefits for the company, as opposed to just a shopping list.

Every company is going to have very clear objectives as to why it wants to work with a charity. These can range from a unique selling proposition against a rival in a competitive marketplace, to achieving a clear stand-out in their commercial sector using the fundraising elements in marketing to generate improved sales and customer acquisition and retention. Partnerships also provide many staff engagement opportunities such as building staff morale through team-working skills and providing volunteering and pro bono opportunities.

The proposal for Save the Children and Mothercare, for example, had obvious synergy with the company's brand but the company also worked in India and China, where Save the Children is extremely active. The proposal was carefully targeted to appeal to their corporate objectives.

UK charities have become much more commercially focused and there is now a strong demand for business people who can bring commercial skills to the third sector."

TOP TIP: "Charities must understand the company's objectives. The charity must be very open and honest and confirm that it can or can't agree to those objectives. If you can't, there's no point trying to fabricate a partnership because the company is going to see through it."

SUMMARY

Dating with a proposal in mind

A compelling proposal is vital to winning the heart and mind of a corporate partner whether you opt for a courtship process, a strategic partnership or a 'Charity of the Year'.

A good pitch should have:

- A strong purpose
- A clear set of objectives
- An understanding of what is needed
- An appreciation of what can be offered
- Win/win

A charity will need to:

- Research the potential partner
- Match the tone and style of the corporate's CR objectives
- Identify a WOW! factor where together you can make a difference
- Use the language of goals and achievement
- Ensure creativity and imagination in the proposal

A corporate will need to:

- Set a clear brief of what is required
- Have a transparent and fair decision-making process
- Give constructive feedback
- Open up the partnership process to lesser-known charities
- Be aware of any costs involved to the charity

TEN-POINT ACTION PLAN		
Action Point 1	Single	Know your purpose
Action Point 2	**Dating**	**Create a compelling proposal ✓**

CHAPTER THREE

Engaged

YOUR PROPOSAL IS ACCEPTED – WHAT NOW?

YOU HAVE SEEN THE BEST OF EACH OTHER – BUT DO YOU REALLY KNOW EACH OTHER?

Securing a charity-corporate partnership is great news. Invariably there will be a time lag between securing a partnership to the actual contractual start date. Think of this time as your engagement – planning for your wedding day!

You will have amassed a lot of information by now. You will be clear on your own purpose, have prepared and presented the proposal and have some thoughts on an overarching goal.

Action Point 3 – "The engagement period" is all about getting to know each other and developing a shared sense of purpose. It is vital at this stage that an honest dialogue develops based on trust and the ability to listen to each other.

"As one of the country's biggest retailers, we have an obligation to give something back to the communities in which we serve. Working with Save the Children has helped us identify where we can have a real impact."

Dalton Philips,
Chief Executive.
Morrisons

"Everyone at Save the Children is thrilled to be working with Morrisons. We have agreed a strategy that delivers a local focus and plays to the strengths of Morrisons."

Douglas Campbell-Rouse,
Corporate Partnerships Director.
Save the Children

FINDINGS:

Engaged – how to agree a joint strategy

John Gray, in his famous book *Men are from Mars, Women are from Venus*, talked about "remembering our differences" and that "good intentions are not enough" – this advice is equally valid for the corporate-charity relationship. Now is the time for honest discussion and real learning and to turn good intentions into action.

Corporates and charities are very different organisations. They will undoubtedly have different values and cultures and ways of working. Bringing together two different organisations to work collaboratively can be challenging.

Joint planning yields greater benefits: The idea of a donor-recipient partnership, with the corporate just viewed as a donor will not yield as many creative ideas as a genuine collaboration. A joint strategy that is widely owned will act as a strong bond between the two organisations.

Getting to know each other is important: The most successful relationships result when two partners know each other well. Time is needed to explore differences, understand each other's aspirations for the partnership and to identify areas of common interest. A good starting point is to refer to your original purpose (see Action Point 1). Go over the proposal again to remind yourselves of what attracted you both together.

Trust in the relationship is critical: Deloitte has done a great deal of work to understand the different partnership models and concluded that those charities and businesses that rise to the challenge of building trust will generate real, lasting value for both parties and for society as a whole. This is not about quick-fix cash injections, but relationships that last, that are innovative and that build capacity and capability on both sides to the benefit of all.

Induction: Partnerships that prepared a good induction process for each other progressed more quickly. Spending time in each other's business, not just the charity's delivery projects, made a real difference in understanding where help was needed and where advice could be offered. Take the time to appreciate each other's values and ways of working.

Knowing what to ask for: A charity might not be aware of all the requests it could make when approaching a corporate. Nor will a corporate be aware of all the challenges the charity was facing when it embarked on its partnership. The engagement phase is the time fully to understand each other's strengths, culture and strategic priorities. By working together and sharing ideas a strong partnership will emerge.

Oxfam and M&S teamed up to help shoppers support the world's poorest people. By just taking old M&S clothes or soft furnishings to an Oxfam shop, people could exchange them for a £5.00 voucher to use back at M&S. This was a simple message to clear out the wardrobe, save money, reduce waste and raise money for Oxfam.

Negotiate mutually beneficial terms: Ensure that the idea of a two-way street is built into the fabric of any joint strategy.

A framework ensures an agreed direction of travel: A joint strategy is not a strict policy that must be tightly adhered to, but it is a strong framework that guides the overall direction and focuses the mind on what can be achieved.

Keep a record of progress: A good tip is to keep a diary all the way through the partnership and provide a comprehensive "lessons learned" paper. This will help you in the future, retain knowledge in case of staff turnover and be a really useful guide for a new partner.

Conclusion: This joint understanding should focus on "WHAT" needs to be achieved and not necessarily on the "HOW" at this stage. It should explore all the possible ways in which the two organisations could support each other. Be bold and look for new and creative solutions to the challenges on which the charity is focused. Widen out the touch points across both organisations. Do not restrict the partnership to the CR and fundraising teams. Great results emerge when a partnership engages the widest possible audience.

CASE HISTORY

Save the Children and Morrisons on agreeing a joint strategy

TOP TIP: "A partnership has to be based on a sound understanding of each other's goals and aspirations, honesty and trust, driven by the joint ambition to succeed."

Douglas Campbell-Rouse,
Corporate Partnerships Director.
Save the Children

Morrisons is the UK's fourth largest food retailer with 470 stores with 11.5 million customers a week. Their business is mainly food and groceries – the weekly shop. To authenticate provenance and maintain quality, Morrisons uniquely sources and processes most of the fresh food they sell through their own manufacturing facilities, and they have more people preparing food in-store than any other retailer. This strategy and focus on quality has ensured Morrisons continues its rapid growth.[5]

The purpose for seeking a charity partner is derived from Morrisons' core business needs. Their growth depends on the communities which are home to their stores, so it is in their interest to ensure that they maximise the value they provide for them. That means being a good employer, a good neighbour and playing an active part in the community.

In searching for a partner Morrisons asked a number of charities to submit proposals which aligned to their local focus. Save the Children successfully won Morrisons' Charity of the Year for 2011 through a staff vote. To help the staff decide, Morrisons asked Save the Children to provide a one-page document and a video explaining the programme and desired outcomes.

Once the partnership was agreed Save the Children and Morrisons set about identifying synergies on which they could build. These included:

- Save the Children's programmes with children and schools in the UK aligned with "Let's Grow" an acclaimed Morrisons' gardening programme in its fourth year inspiring over five million children at 18,000 participating schools.
- Save the Children's work with communities in the UK aligned with Morrisons' values and CR strategy.
- Save the Children's support for families in the UK recognised through their "Different and Better than Ever" approach, was a theme that was at the core of Morrisons' business and objectives

Together Morrisons and Save the Children developed a programme called Families and Schools Together (FAST). This is a UK parental engagement programme which brings the whole community together – children, parents, schools and volunteers – to help families learn together.

FAST supports three-to-eight-year-olds as this is a vital time in children's development. Giving children the chance of a good education is essential to give them the hope of a better future. All children are eager to learn, but for some, their circumstances mean they are up against too many barriers to reach their full potential. The programme can give children better chances at school and make sure the UK's most disadvantaged children get the support they need.

[5] http://www.trtmediasales.co.uk/morrisons-summary#background

Importantly for Morrisons, they are able to support disadvantaged children in the UK in all six of Morrisons' regions. This tangible element to the partnership provides local case studies, local interest and a compelling reason to support Save the Children in their local communities.

Entering into a longer-term partnership was a core objective for Save the Children and an ambition they wanted to include in the joint approach – **not seeing "Charity of the Year" as a barrier to extending the partnership**. Crucially, from the outset, conversation focused on the importance of a longer-term partnership in order for both parties to benefit the most from the relationship. Having this strategic vision negotiated across different tiers of management encouraged Morrisons to review their approach.

Having discussed the benefits of a longer-term more sustainable relationship from the outset, both parties were in a better position to identify clear areas of growth for the partnership that demanded planning and integration into their wider business objectives. This has resulted in the first ever two-year charity partnership for Morrisons. Save the Children hope a successful two-year programme will encourage a third year.

Engaging all the business in the partnership was a key ambition for Morrisons. The joint strategy was all about integrating Save the Children across their business objectives.

In order to achieve this ambition, senior level buy-in was placed at the heart of the partnership. By having a senior advocate in the business it has meant that other directors have become engaged with the charity and partnership in a more dynamic and effective way.

Senior leadership enables honest discussion about frustrations, areas for growth and innovative ideas. This has rapidly increased the efficiency of the partnership, decisions are made more quickly and project groups are formed for planning.

Having the partnership located across all areas of the business has in this instance, enabled greater cross-departmental working and has encouraged integration into marketing, promotional and communications planning for the year ahead across the wider business. This is much more effective than when the relationship is confined to the CR department.

Providing a multi-faceted partnership has enabled the alignment of both charity and company objectives – **campaigns, policy, advocacy and global emergency support** – and has enabled several benefits to emerge, including:

- Sponsorship of Save the Children's Party Conference activities – as well as sponsorship, senior directors from Morrisons joining the panel of speakers discussing Save the Children's work in the UK and asking the political parties to take notice.

- Sponsorship of a major TV show – as part of the "No Child Born to Die" campaign sponsoring ITV1's Born to Shine, a joint ITV1 and Save the Children venture – giving talented children the opportunity to teach celebrities a new skill. Morrisons had never before sponsored a major TV programme.
- Support of Save the Children's Born to Shine Roadshows – delivered at ten Morrisons' locations across the UK to bring the ITV1 show to life. This gave children the opportunity to shine in their local communities and increased footfall to Morrisons' stores, helping to reinforce the benefits of the partnership.
- Engagement with communities involved in the recent riots to provide early intervention in a community that needs support.
- Responding to emergencies – Morrisons have acted quickly to support Save the Children's response to global emergencies, therefore riding the wave of public interest in the UK, giving customers the opportunity to support through collections.

Cause-related marketing (CRM) opportunities in-store that align to business objectives and major campaigns are jointly explored. The partnership launched with a Unilever CRM promotion, generating significant funds over a number of their brands. Save the Children has been given the opportunity to feed into Morrisons' 2012 plans for in-store promotions due to the extension of the partnership. By providing key campaign moments and ideas, the partnership is exploring delivering a significant presence in-store to generate as much funding and awareness as possible.

ACTION POINT 3:

Take the time to understand each other's strengths, culture and strategic priorities. Allow creative ideas and innovation to flow as you understand exactly what each other is trying to achieve. Look at all the areas where a partnership can make an impact beyond simply handing out money.

Engaged – Agree a joint strategy

The ideas and expectations discussed in the proposal now have to turn into achievable realistic goals that both organisations can commit to and deliver.

It is not until the partnership is actually agreed on that both sides can really start to talk and generate new ideas.

Getting to know each other establishes a strong starting point for the partnership. Creating the environment that allows trust and creativity to flourish is important. An honest dialogue helps explore where the real value lies in this new partnership.

Action Point 3 is not meant to imply that once a joint strategy is written it cannot bend and flex to reflect changes. On the contrary, it should build in ideas generation and encourage regular dialogue. This time is about a show of togetherness, it sets the tone for how your relationship will grow and evolve.

An issue to factor in at this stage is the current and past relationships of both new partners. On the corporate side, is there a current charity partner which you are replacing? If so, what you can learn from them? (see chapter 9). Try and get time with the outgoing partner and look at what worked well. This engagement period may be challenging if the outgoing partner is focused on that last-minute push to squeeze every last inch out of that relationship. Thought should be given to the change-over period.

No matter how experienced both partners are, a good communication process and an engagement strategy will be needed to help colleagues either to make a switch from a past charity partner and/or develop a new allegiance.

Think of giving each other a crash induction course to develop an understanding of each other's cultures and organisational values. A key point of contact for each organisation must be selected to have an oversight of everything that is going on and to be the route in for enquiries and ideas. It is a good idea to spend time in each other's organisations and get to know the workings of each other's business.

Focus heavily on the "WHAT has to be achieved".

Bupa's stated purpose is "to help people live longer, healthier, happier lives", it looked for a charity "with a focus on keeping people well", that helps people get more active and to take steps to be healthier. The Alzheimer's Society matched this aim perfectly; together they agreed areas of work where they could make a real impact. Bupa's partnership with The Alzheimer's Society raised nearly £4 million.

SECRETS TO SUCCESS

Togetherness – getting to know each other

The key is developing a bespoke approach together – Make sure you link this to the specific needs of the charity and the corporate.

Exercise:

What do you really know about each other? Plan an induction course for each other. Prepare a briefing note on each organisation that can be shared by all colleagues of both organisations. Aspire to have 100% of people in both organisations to have an awareness of your partnership – not just key personnel.

What are you going to focus on? You need to discuss the purpose of each organisation and to bring these together under clear headings that are jointly agreed. You need to let each other into the heart of your operations to see where you can make the most impact.

What do you both want to achieve? Remember to focus on the WHAT and not the HOW. Powerful, mutually beneficial partnerships are emerging that bring enhanced benefits for business, charities and wider society. Identify why you are stronger together.

What will success look like? How will you know you are delivering? What are you both expecting the partnership to deliver? Some measures are easy to identify, such as the number of volunteers, employee engagement and amounts raised. Other deliverables are harder to measure. Look at reducing cost, improving skills and raising brand profile as essential factors to success.

What are your strengths and weaknesses? What can you do to best complement each other? Many of the case studies used in this guide talk of synergies and complementary objectives. It is important to work on areas where there is a joint goal.

What touch points exist already? A good first exercise is to map if you have any contact points. Do any of your colleagues already support the charity? Do any of your key customers or clients support the charity? Search out any natural champions. A partnership can be enhanced by widening the reach to the supply chain and customer base.

THOMAS HUGHES-HALLETT

Chief Executive Marie Curie Cancer Care, discusses what makes a successful partnership

"Creating a successful charity partnership has three fundamental elements: effective planning, having the right person or team in place, and sustainability.

A strong partnership that will strengthen over time starts with a clear vision of what the partnership wants to achieve. Does the corporate want to engage customers with their local community, raise awareness of key issues, engage their workforce with one another or perhaps, and most likely, a combination of all of these? To do this, you need to be clear about the objectives of the partnership and clearly define the outcomes that you want, making sure they are realistic and achievable. The partnership must be easy for everyone to understand and accessible to all.

The very best corporate partnerships infiltrate every corner of an organisation and are embraced by everyone who works with, or is impacted by, the company. Agreeing a joint strategy and a theme that is important to your customers and staff, such as community support, health or education will enable people to galvanise around the partnership objectives. A joint strategy helps ensure a simple clear communication message, tangible goals and a sustainable partnership. Charities must be clear about the amount of income they want to fundraise. Ensure you interrogate the corporate partner to confirm they can support your plans. Be clear where sharing of expertise can add real benefit and where value can be added.

Once you are clear on your joint objectives you need to find the right people to make it happen. The individual or team who manages the partnership needs to understand both organisations, the culture of charity support, how to engage staff and customers and have a keen eye for identifying partnership opportunities in every area of your organisation. Someone who has worked in the organisation for a while and understands the culture will be ideal.

At the end of the day, it's your staff and customers who will really make the partnership a success so it's vital that whoever is managing the partnership communicates your objectives clearly. Keep any messaging simple and ensure everyone understands the personal difference their input will make.

A large number of charity partnerships only last a year, but the most effective partnerships are the ones that provide continual support for a charity or have a legacy beyond the initial partnership period. Providing sustainable support will allow charities to plan for the long term more effectively. The legacy of any partnership should be brought into the planning right from the beginning and should be explored as part of the joint strategic approach."

TOP TIP: "Effective planning helps build the right relationship. A great partnership is exactly that; it's a union between an organisation and a charity that will help both to achieve their goals."

SUMMARY

Perfect engagement party

A joint strategy will enable everyone from both organisations to share a common sense of purpose and know what the partnership hopes to achieve. It helps articulate the shared objectives and should be a platform for inspiring ideas and encouraging engagement.

A joint strategy will have:

- Clear aims and objectives
- An understanding of success
- Areas of common interest
- A time-line
- A review process

Ensure that together you:

- Create opportunities to get to know each other
- Extend the induction process across both organisations
- Build trust between the key people managing the partnership
- Explore all the areas where value could be added
- Take on board each other's points of view

TEN-POINT ACTION PLAN		
Action Point 1	Single	Know your purpose
Action Point 2	Dating	Create a compelling proposal
Action Point 3	**Engaged**	**Agree a joint strategy** ✓

CHAPTER FOUR

Vows

PREPARING FOR THE BIG DAY – DO YOU KNOW WHAT YOUR WEDDING VOWS MEAN?

FOR BETTER OR WORSE!

This guide offers a passionate belief in the value that a good charity-corporate partnership can generate. It is critical, however, that any partnership is based on some kind of written agreement.

A relationship can of course take many forms: a fling, a casual affair, living together, an open marriage, or a longer-term, more dedicated, relationship. A charity-corporate partnership can bring many benefits. However, without the correct preparation, they have the potential to bring problems and conflicts. Action Point 4 is all about being clear on the nature of your relationship. The excitement of WHAT could be achieved also needs to be tempered at this stage with the consideration of legal advice, tax and VAT advice.

Benjamin Franklin said: "It takes many good deeds to build a good reputation, and only one bad one to lose it." Commercial partnerships which do not represent a good deal for a charity can damage the reputation of charities in general by giving the impression that charities are willing to become involved in commercial ventures even if there is little financial benefit to be derived.

"Charities need to make certain that the proposed commercial agreement represents a fair deal for the charity. Additionally, it is recommended that charities should familiarise themselves with the good practice guidance available, prior to entering into an agreement."

Taken from the Charity Commission "Charities and Commercial Partners" (RS2) (July 2002).

"Without the correct preparation, charity-corporate partnerships have the potential to bring with them problems and conflicts. Much will depend on how the relationship is set up and the preparation undertaken right at the beginning."

Taken from the Institute of Fundraising Code of Practice "Charities Working with Business".

FINDINGS:

Vows – how formal does a partnership need to be?

Good practice guidelines from respected organisations, such as the Institute of Fundraising, strongly recommend the drawing up of a written agreement. Some corporates have straightforward memorandums of association, others have more complex cause-related marketing agreements.

Process for due diligence: Action Point 1 was all about knowing your purpose and, from a charity perspective, this should involve developing a policy on how to engage the corporate sector. This policy should be agreed and owned by the trustees. For example, an "avoidance" list of companies may be drawn up (such as a cancer charity not wanting to accept donations from a tobacco company). This may seem straightforward, but it is important that there is a process for carrying out due diligence on potential partners, especially as companies often have much larger parent companies. Being in a position to research potential partners is important. A corporate will also want to carry out due diligence on the financial viability of the charity's activities.

Type of agreement: Once a potential partnership has been agreed, both partners must clarify how the relationship will be managed and delivered. This can be anything from a simple memorandum of understanding to a complex cause-related marketing agreement. Most partnerships researched for this guide had a simple "letter of commitment".

Donation/funding: It is helpful to be clear if there is to be a minimum donation irrespective of any fundraising (which is more difficult to quantify). It is helpful to manage expectations in this respect.

Programme outline: It is helpful to determine the programme and areas of work. New ideas may well emerge as the partnership progresses, but both partners should have a base line of what they are delivering.

Statistics and impact: It is useful to give a top-line indication of the data that will be captured and how the impact of the partnership will be recorded and reported. You may wish to consider where the agreement for success is best positioned. Success measures can be agreed as part of the joint strategy (see Action Point 3). No one can predict the actual final fundraising amounts and the contract need not be specific. The agreement should, however, make it clear what is expected of both parties by way of sharing information and data. An agreement may wish to specify a minimum donation by way of covering any costs or expenses that a charity may incur in starting up a new corporate partnership. The corporate can be asked to underwrite certain activities to protect a charity from losing money on a project.

Process for decision making: There needs to be an agreed written process for decision making. Chapter 5 discusses the need for a clear structure for managing the operational issues but there also needs to be contractual accountability. Delegated authority needs to be made clear. As the partnership progresses many decisions will be taken that will be value judgements and much excitement will overtake the proceedings. All those with management responsibility should be clear on boundaries and who can make final decisions.

Management structure: The structure that is put in place to manage the partnership should also be outlined in the agreement. The key personnel overseeing the partnership will use the joint strategy and the written agreement as a guide on all activities. This process will help keep a fair and equitable balance in the relationship. Should a disagreement arise and one partner wishes to leave, then you will need to be able to refer to the agreement for support.

Manage conflicts of interest: Partnerships will result from common interests and the desire to work well together. You should be clear where any conflicts of interest may occur as there is often a fine line between the two. There are a range of questions to be worked through such as:

- What would a charity do if a potential corporate partner supplied products, goods or services to an area that was core to your charity – such as a pharmaceutical company working alongside an AIDS foundation?
- What would you do if a corporate wanted an exclusive partnership?
- Trustees and Non-Executive Directors are often very useful at generating contacts with corporates – how will you manage any undue influence and conflicts of interests?

Risk assessments and red tape can stifle a corporate relationship and it will be a challenge to manage this process. You will need to have someone on the joint team who can manage risks, especially those associated with fundraising.

Transparency and governance: Misuse of funds must be guarded against. You must have a clear contractual process for managing all funds raised, especially if this involves the public. Many corporates now fundraise for national events such as Children in Need. For example, Post Office Ltd has raised over £1.5 million in the last three years, the vast amount of which has come from public donations. Having a process which provides transparency and due diligence is paramount to retaining public confidence in your charity brand. In chapter 1 we talked about the value of a charity brand – there is simply no room for scandal where donations are concerned. Post Office Ltd, for example, accounted for all the public donations for Barnardo's through its own cash-management process and engaged a third party professional organisation, Charities Trust, to process the money. The public must know at all times exactly how much is being raised and for what.

Branding: The agreement must cover issues such as the use of each other's branding and logo. Who will own the branding of events and products? Barnardo's, for example, owns its brand of "The Big Toddle" and various partners have acted as sponsors including Lloyds Banking Group and Royal Mail Group. It is important that the contract covers how the partnership will be presented to the outside world. This is especially true when public donations accrue. For example, if a partnership agrees to retail a Christmas card in aid of its charity partner it must be clear who is doing what and how much of the revenue will be transferred to the charity. A great deal of thought should be given to how PR and marketing will use the charity-corporate partnership. It should be clear who can do what and who has the final sign-off on branding issues. This relates also to press releases and media events. Again, having a joint managing structure will really help with ensuring the agreement is adhered to.

Liabilities: As well as the value judgements and decisions that will be taken to generate fundraising activities, The Charities Act 2006 puts commitments on both the charity and the corporate partner. Where financial gain is evident then each partner must comply with the VAT rules and taxable gains from trading activities. The law states that there must be a written agreement that governs any charity-corporate partnership and any trading subsidiary. The tax and VAT rules can be a bit tricky in this area and expert advice should be sought. Put simply – if there is a benefit to be received then tax liability will accrue. The problem with VAT is that, if no VAT is charged and then it is subsequently decided that it is due, the charity will then have to pay the VAT and will therefore benefit from less revenue. This can be further complicated if dealing with a corporate that is not VAT rated such as a bank.

A simple charitable donation is less fraught with complications. However, as we have discussed, the days of a corporate simply wanting to write a cheque are coming to an end. There are varied benefits to both parties and in these instances tax and VAT may be involved. Most agreements will need to be approved with the legal teams and care should be taken to stay on the right side of the Charity Act. This can be even more complicated if more than one charity is involved. It should also be noted that regulations differ between England, Wales and Scotland.

Conclusion: It is usual to have a letter of agreement setting, out expectations under broad headings as indicated above. It is not advisable to just leave a partnership to chance and goodwill. There is a great deal of advice on this more complex side of the charity-corporate relationship. The Institute of Fundraising and the Charity Commission both offer templates, codes of practice and guidance. An address directory is provided on pages 103-107 of this guide.[6]

[6] The authors of this guide are not lawyers or tax advisors and you should always consult professionals to ensure Step 4 in the Action Plan is completed thoroughly. The Institute of Fundraising and the Charity Commission have both produced guidelines on drawing up a contract to help manage charity-corporate relationships.

CASE HISTORY

Save the Children and Reckitt Benckiser had a strong agreement underpinning their relationship

Reckitt Benckiser (RB) is a world leader in household, health and personal care. The company employs about 27,000 people worldwide, with operations in more than 60 countries and sales in almost 200 countries. RB is the company behind a huge range of well-known household brands, including Dettol, Nurofen, Vanish, Finish and Harpic.

RB chose Save the Children as their charity partner, aligning their partnership agreement around three common goals:

- Global presence
- Support for families
- Health and hygiene

Clear objectives were agreed so that they knew what was expected of each other:

- To improve the lives of some of the world's poorest children
- To raise significant funds, with clear financial targets set each year
- To be a leading example of a long-term, strategic partnership
- To engage RB employees around the globe
- To raise awareness of Save the Children's work and RB's commitment to CR

In early 2011, RB launched the "Million Brighter Futures" campaign, pledging to raise £10 million for Save the Children by 2015, and create a million brighter futures for children.

The agreement between the two organisations was based on:

- Clear partnership objectives
- Commitment to fundraising targets, with progress regularly monitored
- Bespoke Save the Children account management team, resourced appropriately
- Management at a senior level within RB
- Global and local focus
- Open, honest communication and a flexible approach
- Proactively developing new, innovative ways to engage with employees
- Working as a true partnership – absolute key to the success!

TOP TIP: "A clear agreement on areas of work provides clarity and a basis from which to work. It is important to manage everyone's expectations on what the partnership can deliver."

Douglas Campbell-Rouse,
Corporate Partnerships Director
Save the Children

ACTION POINT 4:

Formalising a charity-corporate partnership helps protect both partners. It provides for a sensible framework to help manage expectations and ensure the partnership stays on track.

Vows – Secure a written agreement

Agree the overarching terms of the partnership in a written agreement. The overall potential value of the partnership will influence the strength of the contract.

Set out the process for good governance and transparency. A charity-corporate partnership can be worth £ millions in new revenue to a charity; due diligence over funding is essential.

There must be a strict adherence to the law, due diligence around managing the money and respect in dealing with people. A corporate-charity relationship is, to all intents and purposes, driven forward by a desire to make a difference. Outcomes are delivered by harnessing the goodwill of people, whether that is through fundraising, volunteering or pro bono expertise. There are, however, legal and financial ramifications of such actions, make sure these are taken into account.

The agreement should also protect the ethics of a charity-corporate partnership.

Many activities that emerge from such a relationship will incur a cost, such as the use of the brand logo, materials, buildings and such assets. Some activities will engage the general public. It is important to have an understanding if any of these costs can be underwritten by the corporate partner or recouped from public donations.

An agreement helps set the boundaries when using branding and logos. It helps avoid any misunderstanding when issuing press statements. It provides transparency for trustees and directors.

This does not have to be a complex legal contract covering every conceivable project that is seen as a possible hindrance. It can be a simple memorandum of understanding, but it is unwise to agree a partnership without a sound contractual understanding.

A good memorandum of understanding will set out the main issues on use of the brand, financial transparency, review process, accountability, and duration of the partnership, liability issues, clarity on tax and VAT and the ethical boundaries.

Mind has a very clear position published on its web site which sets out the principles upon which it will work with a corporate partner. It holds firm to its ethical stance on working with pharmaceutical companies and has a clear policy on product endorsement. Mind were chosen as Veolia Environmental Services first ever charity partner and they have a clear understanding on how they will work together.

SECRETS TO SUCCESS

For better or worse – agreeing your vows

You will need to give a clear brief to the procurement/legal teams to ensure an agreement that finds the right balance between protection to both parties and flexibility to generate new ideas.

Exercise:

Have you a process in place for completing due diligence? Whenever a partnership is proposed it is important to understand why such a partnership would offer benefit. Both parties must go through a process of due diligence to identify any risks that the proposed partnership could bring. Research needs to extend to parent companies and in some cases supply-chain practices.

Do you have the expertise to produce an agreement? Who is responsible for ensuring this process happens smoothly and without delay? The written agreement must ensure compliance with the relevant fundraising legislation and the Charities Act. The agreement must seek to protect the brand integrity of both parties and ensure the ethical considerations of any charity are not put at risk.

Have you a defined policy in place on working as a charity-corporate partnership? There must be a process for decision making. This should make clear delegated responsibilities and who can sign off communications, especially press releases and use of the brand logo. What do both parties expect to gain from the relationship? What process will you set up to monitor and review progress? It is important that the agreement recognises the ethical policy of the charity.

What happens should a severe disagreement take place? Who has the final say and who is ultimately responsible? The agreement should provide for an exit strategy should it be needed.

What will the process be for completing risk assessments – where will responsibility lie? Colleagues can be extremely creative and ambitious in fundraising. It is important that there is a process and appropriate insurance in place to manage activities.

How long will the partnership last? The agreement will need to deal with the duration of the partnership and how it will come to an end.

Exclusive relationship or multiple partners? The agreement should be clear on exclusivity, access to donor data-bases, what is going to be said about the partnership and indeed if there can be more than one partner involved.

When will funds be paid over? Nearly all charities seek a partnership in order to raise funds. The agreement needs to specify when and how monies raised will be handed over.

There are many such questions to be explored and it is advisable to seek advice. The Charities Aid Foundation, Institute of Fundraising and the Charity Commission all provide advice and guidance on managing a formal written agreement.

JONATHAN EVANS

Partner at Linklaters LLP, shares his thoughts on the importance of a contractual understanding

"Marriage vows are traditionally recited by the parties in public and not reduced to writing, although they will often now be recorded for posterity by the ubiquitous camcorder. However, no one would doubt the force of those vows despite their not being recorded in writing. Although not often appreciated, much the same can be said about commercial contracts and partnerships. Just because the relationship is not distilled in writing does not mean it does not legally exist and does not constitute an enforceable contract. Even without a formal written contract, more often than not the relationship will still be given the force of law and enforced by the courts, based, for example, on what the courts presume the intention of the parties was when entering into the arrangements. Even if the major terms of the deal are reduced to writing, the courts or legislation may fill in any gaps by implying terms into the parties' agreement.

Given this, arriving at a contractual understanding between the parties may seem of reduced importance if the law will step in and define it for them; but as so often is the case in a relationship, unless issues are discussed explicitly then the parties' views can remain at odds but hidden. Such divergent views only become apparent when the relationship is in trouble. Inevitably, when a conflict occurs either one party's view of the arrangements is upheld leaving the other disappointed, or the law imposes an alternative interpretation on the arrangement leaving both unhappy.

This makes the importance of reducing the parties' contractual understanding to writing more important and the parties should strive to do so at the outset in a way that is as comprehensive as possible. This is particularly important where one party comes from the third sector and the other is a commercial organisation; they are much more likely to have very different perceptions of their relationship.

Reducing the relationship to a written agreement will not only provide evidence of the relationship and its terms but it will also help the parties define it. The very process of drafting a comprehensive agreement will force both parties to determine and explain their objectives in entering into the relationship and what they expect the other party to do in return. It will also force them to address issues both may not have contemplated, such as the breakdown of the relationship or how it is to end. Rather than highlight the potential problems in the relationship, however, the process of agreeing a comprehensive contract should enable both parties to ensure that they control the future of the relationship and have greater confidence that it will be successful for both of them.

Hopefully, if the agreement is properly drawn up, it will be the foundation of a successful partnership and then, rather like so many recordings of a marriage ceremony, it will not need to be looked at with regret."

SUMMARY

Writing your vows

A written agreement helps to draw the boundaries of any charity-corporate partnership. The agreement is there to provide a safety net and help mitigate against risks.

An agreement should have:

- Clarity on the financial expectation/minimum donation
- A broad programme of work
- Review processes for monitoring activities
- Communications and intellectual property rights
- Termination clause – notice period

Both charity and corporate must be clear on the following areas:

- Accountability and responsibility for decision making
- Due diligence and transparency regarding money raised
- Compliance with fundraising legislation
- Ethical implications for the charity
- Clarity around underwriting of costs

TEN-POINT ACTION PLAN		
Action Point 1	Single	Know your purpose
Action Point 2	Dating	Create a compelling proposal
Action Point 3	Engaged	Agree a joint strategy
Action Point 4	**Vows**	**Draw up a written agreement** ✓

CHAPTER FIVE

Honeymoon

MARRIED – HOW IMPORTANT IS A GOOD HONEYMOON?

WHO WEARS THE TROUSERS?

You already know quite a lot about your own purpose and what you want to achieve together. Creating the right environment will help you focus on how the strategy will be delivered.

Action Point 5 focuses on leadership and a strong management structure to provide the best possible environment to deliver the joint strategy.

"In order to maximise the success of the partnership it was critical that the senior management team at both Tesco and Whizz-Kidz supported the partnership from the top down."

Ruth Girardet,
CR and Communities Director.
Tesco

"Having a proper structure to manage the relationship, including the regular sharing of ideas at senior level as well as on the ground is essential."

Heather Hancock,
Managing Partner for Innovation.
Deloitte

"Senior leadership cements the partnership on day one and drives the speed at which you can make decisions and deliver. Reporting back to senior leaders focuses everyone's mind."

Gary Grange,
Community Investment Manager.
Royal Mail

FINDINGS:

Honeymoon – how to ensure early success

All partnerships are organic and evolve as more people become engaged with their purposes. Leadership sets the tone of the relationship. It guides ambition and helps embed the partnership right across organisational structures. Senior leadership raises the stakes and moves CR from the sidelines to centre stage.

Strengthens relationships: It is important that the leaders of both organisations give the partnership attention and that they connect with each other. The visibility of CEOs from the charity and the corporate working together has a massive impact on engaging senior managers across the business. This joint leadership at the very top strengthens relationships throughout the partnership.

Added value: Leadership really adds value, especially if conflict arises or in cases where the relationship is not equitable. For example, feedback from charities suggested occasional nervousness on the part of a charity in pushing back on a corporate if the demand was too great or if a project was going to create a "mission drift". Requests included corporates' unrealistic assumption that the charity partners could produce a celebrity on demand. A conversation between the two CEOs is capable of unlocking any sticking points.

Connects the business case: The involvement of the corporate CEO makes a real difference to the overall success of a partnership, especially as they really understand the overall strategic business goals. They have the ability to see synergies and understand how to leverage relationships. Their support can add a level of sophistication to a partnership and they have the decision-making capacity to think the impossible.

Unsurprisingly, where there is senior leadership for CR in a corporate you are more likely to see specific industry challenges linked to the CR agenda. For example:

- Easyjet have linked with carbon offset charities and offer each customer the chance to pay £3.00 extra to offset their carbon footprint.
- Sainsbury's support responsible retailing and have a strategic alliance with Fair Trade companies.
- Divine Chocolate emerged as an ethically sourced product.
- BSkyB has used the power of their commercial proposition to raise awareness of WWF to highlight the rainforest situation.
- Fujitsu are using their core expertise to help with digital inclusion and accessibility for disabled people.

Market leading companies will concentrate on what they do best. Deloitte, in their report, "More than just giving"[7] note that this trend is useful for charities to capitalise on. CEOs will want to understand how a partnership can support a cause using its core expertise.

Charities need to understand where their own core proposition aligns to a corporate's core business and to capitalise on this when preparing their proposal.

[7] "More Than Just Giving. Analysis of Corporate Responsibility across UK Firms" (2011), www.deloitte.com.

Engages specialist areas: Directors of specialist areas can be engaged more easily when there is an impact on their own strategic area. Human resources professionals will be interested in how they can use CR to attract and retain talent. Graduates are becoming increasingly inquisitive on corporate reputational impact and are searching out companies that offer opportunities for volunteering. Public affairs directors will be interested in how they can leverage a conversation with Government. Sales and marketing teams will be interested in supplier and customer relationships and where there might be relationships through charity partners.

Networking: Charities need to understand this business rationale in engaging with the CR agenda. Understanding that leadership plays a crucial role should drive the desire to foster relationships with senior people. Non-Executive Directors and trustees can play a pivotal role in making introductions.

Motivational: There is strong evidence to back up the view that senior leaders are interested in the benefits of the CR agenda. BITC conducted a poll amongst business leaders in 2010, the results of which indicated that 67% of business leaders believe that a more responsible economy is going to emerge from the recession, and nearly all (97%) believe that individual business leaders must be seen to act to restore confidence in business.

Equal partners: The arena of CR is becoming more professional, business leaders see it as integral to their own business strategy and the economy of such partnerships is evolving. What charities must ensure is a real balance of power in these relationships. The corporate relationship should not result in mission drift. The charity partner should not feel that they have to marry for money or accept volunteering programmes that do not add real value. It is equally essential that the charity's leadership has the strength to remain true to core ethics and values.

Management structure: As well as strong leadership, having a clear structure for managing a partnership was also a critical factor raised by the case studies in this guide. There are variations on the management process, from Teenage Cancer Trust who prefer to embed a colleague within their corporate partner (chapter 6) to Save the Children who have a process using senior account managers (chapter 3). Having a clear structure for managing the partnership removes barriers and supports true engagement.

Conclusion: The key advice in this guide is to create a structure that has authority to make a difference and drive forward the passion and commitment. This requires a much wider skill set than just fundraising.

CASE HISTORY

Royal Mail Group and Barnardo's on the importance of leadership and structure

TOP TIP: "Visible top-level commitment can often be a turning point in garnering support from every part of the organisation, keep the leadership team informed with regular updates and ask for their input."

Gary Grange,
Community Investment Manager.
Royal Mail Group

Royal Mail Group and Barnardo's are two of the UK's most recognisable brands, each with a strong sense of purpose and place in the local community. The scale and history of these organisations brought challenges when trying to establish the partnership.

Getting to know each other and agreeing joint objectives took longer than was anticipated. Connecting the two CEOs was a pivotal moment in clarifying objectives and driving the partnership forward. They instigated a senior leadership dinner with directors from both organisations. This meeting produced greater clarity around key actions and an agreement to a more structured management approach.

A Charity Partnership Board was created, chaired by the Company Secretary. This board was made up of senior people from across Royal Mail Group and Barnardo's who could influence and deliver the actions at a faster pace. The Charity Partnership Board met monthly and had a clear focus on reporting back on progress. This process drove a new approach to internal communications.

Ownership from senior leaders resulted in much wider business engagement. A joint strategy was published that moved away from just fundraising. Eight areas of work were agreed. Success indicators were then monitored against these eight areas with monthly update reports.

Sharing expertise became a key focus of the joint strategy. For example, Royal Mail Media Centre supported Barnardo's in the design and delivery of an award-winning Direct Mail Campaign, the HR teams helped Barnardo's with their shared services, and the retail division helped with the high-street shops. A key output of the relationship was the delivery of a work programme which saw over 100 young people mentored into the world of work.

The sheer scale of embedding the partnership across such a large complex organisation required planning and strong communications. From generating sustainable payroll-giving every month, to a one-off effort focusing on a month of fundraising, engaging colleagues in volunteering, and supporting Barnardo's campaign messages at party conferences, the partnership covered a lot of ground.

The partnership lasted over three years, with over 80% of the fleet carrying the "Proud to Support Barnardo's" logo, the partnership raised over £2 million and generated £45,000 every month from payroll-giving.

ACTION POINT 5:

Leadership and a clear management structure at the beginning of the partnership will ensure the relationship exists for mutual benefit. Commitment from the senior leadership will help embed the partnership across both organisations leading to wider engagement.

Honeymoon – Secure top-level commitment
When any charity partnership is formed it is likely that one partner will be more experienced, larger, have higher expectations and want different levels of commitment. Bringing together different cultures and value sets will be challenging.

Secure the commitment from senior leaders to act as a catalyst from which individual passion and commitment will follow. Leadership sets the tone and style of CR for any business and moves social action from the sidelines to centre stage.

Establish a clear structure for managing the partnership for delivering on the day-to-day aspects of the relationship. Having the right people in place within this structure is so important. Being able to understand each other's objectives helps manage any issues which could potentially impact negatively on a charity partner. Equally it helps a charity understand the needs of a corporate.

A successful partnership is one where there are not rigid constraints that stifle new ideas but a clear process that allows speedy sign-off for decisions. Protecting the brand of both organisations is really important, refer back to the agreement and sign-off process, leadership and structure to get the approval needed for delivering ideas.

For example, The British Red Cross and Tesco have had a successful partnership – there have been instances where the charity has presented ideas, but Tesco knew from experience what would work and what would not in their retail environment. What is important is that there is an honest two-way process for developing and agreeing ideas.

United Utilities (UU) Executive Leadership Team (ELT) worked with their community charity partner, WaterAid, to provide essential facilities for a village school in Zambia. The ELT were sent to the Monze district to build a block of toilets for the school and community. United Utilities customers take clean water and sanitation for granted. The leadership at UU wanted to drive forward a project that would have real impact on a community that did not have access to these basic facilities.

SECRETS TO SUCCESS

Meet the relatives – a meeting of minds

John Gray in his book points out that "Men and women are generally unaware that they have different emotional needs. As a result they do not instinctively know how to support each other". Corporates and charities will naturally have different value sets and the secret to success is in creating a structure that enables a supportive relationship.

Exercise:

How will you engage your senior leaders? Once you have your partnership in place you need to set about arranging for the two CEOs to have a meeting. This is an excellent first starting point. A joint statement from these two individuals to both organisations helps anchor the relationship and send a signal of commitment. A simple photo-call of the two CEOs together is a great launch pad for the communication strategy which will follow.

How will the partnership be managed? Ensure you have a clear structure in place to manage the partnership and review progress. There are several models presented in this guide for you to think through. You should publish the agreed structure during your communication process so that everyone in the organisation can connect to the partnership teams.

How will you ensure an effective sign-off process? Within the partnership management structure you must name the individuals who can sign off on decisions, especially those decisions involving use of the brand logos.

How will you communicate transparency and governance? This subject will be covered in your agreement, which will stipulate how money must be transferred. It is vital that colleagues and the public know exactly how funds raised are being transferred to the chosen charity. This will be even more important if funds are generated from cause-related marketing and sale of products. Honesty and transparency must govern all communications.

How are the day-to-day operations managed? Having experienced people running the day-to-day relationship is just as important as engaging your senior leaders. Make sure you don't put all the effort into the dating game and then delegate down for the partnership phase. The account managers are the face of your partnership and have to be able to build relationships.

How will you ensure an equal relationship? Take time to reflect on each other's needs. Arrange visits to each other's organisations with structured inductions. Make sure both partners have an equal voice at the decision-making and ideas-generation stages. If the charity is a much smaller voice, think through what support you can offer.

STEPHEN HOWARD

CEO of Business in the Community has a unique insight into the minds of business leaders

"Passion, determination and drive are vital elements of good leadership. At Business in the Community we have a powerful tool to inspire dynamic CEOs to involve their company in charity partnerships. Charities and businesses working together is about more than just philanthropy. There is always a tendency to read business involvement with charities as just another form of marketing and for voluntary sector groups to view business as a cash cow. Deep, sustainable and true partnerships can release all kinds of benefits for both sides.

Business leaders bring a whole range of skills, experience and new resources to the voluntary sector. They have the necessary clout to imbed the CR agenda throughout their companies. If charity partnerships are to be successful they have to matter outside of the CEO's office, but igniting the chief executive's passion is a good place to start and it can be a really effective catalyst to start the ball rolling, as my own story attests all too well...

I had recently been appointed into my first Chief Executive role of a FTSE company and we had just moved our headquarters to a building off the Strand, overlooking the River Thames with stunning views of St Paul's Cathedral and Parliament. On all fronts, I was riding high! However, behind this wonderful building, some 50 rough sleepers regularly congregated nightly as they had nowhere else to go. Clearly this was impossible to ignore and I felt the need to do something. At about the same time, in 1998, I was invited on one of The Prince of Wales' Seeing is Believing visits, which was a first-hand exposure to the problems and issues faced by homeless people in the capital. We kept reconvening and further considering the problems we had heard and looked at potential solutions. Thus began Business in the Community's Business Action on Homelessness campaign and more than 2,000 people have been found sustained employment through the programme.

Leadership is critical, but to achieve deep and sustained impact partnership is vital. An example of a long-term partnership arrangement is Project Shoreditch, a partnership between East London Business Alliance (ELBA), Hammerson, UBS, British Land, and Linklaters which has helped grassroots organisations effectively to address priority issues including crime, health, access to employment and learning. Since 2005, the project has facilitated over 7,500 employee volunteers and provided support to over 125 local organisations and enterprises. Employee volunteering is an excellent way to get buy-in from across the organisation and give your staff development opportunities.

I have seen some truly impressive work and lives changed when companies and charities work together and I am so pleased to see that corporate appetite has not been dampened despite the downturn. Companies want to commit to do more and 77% of our business leaders agreed that they could do more to scale-up strategic support for communities across their business."

TOP TIP: "Tapping into business leadership should be seen as a vital opportunity for any charity. Business leaders have a great deal of talent and energy and can help develop opportunities that the third sector working in isolation would find hard to achieve."

SUMMARY

Building a close relationship

An engaged leadership team will bring an energy and commitment to a partnership and help widen the partnership's impact across both organisations. Close relationships between key personnel is essential as these people are passionate advocates and negotiators who deliver the outcomes.

Ensure both partners:

- Secure visible senior leadership
- Agree a clear structure for managing the partnership
- Have experienced people running the day-to-day operations
- Respect each other's motives
- Understand each other's organisations

The outcome should be:

- Clear and realistic expectations
- Honest dialogue
- Idea generation
- Better decision-making
- The ability to manage any changes in key personnel

TEN-POINT ACTION PLAN		
Action Point 1	Single	Know your purpose
Action Point 2	Dating	Create a compelling proposal
Action Point 3	Engaged	Agree a joint strategy
Action Point 4	Vows	Draw up a written agreement
Action Point 5	**Honeymoon**	**Secure top-level commitment** ✓

CHAPTER SIX

Marriage

THE HONEYMOON IS OVER – NOW YOU HAVE TO LIVE TOGETHER

HOW DO YOU MAKE A MARRIAGE REALLY WORK SO BOTH PARTNERS ARE TRULY HAPPY?

Passion, fun and excitement are at the heart of a strong relationship. You now have to help create the right environment to let the relationship grow. Campaigns should aim to inform, inspire and engage people in the charity cause.

Capturing the hearts and minds of colleagues will drive engagement, generate ideas and inspire people to want to be involved.

Action Point 6 is all about HOW you will make this partnership a success.

"It's all about 'horses for courses'. You have to invest in every relationship to reap the rewards. It's about spotting the potential, being flexible and adapting your approach to match your partner."

Simon Davies,
CEO.
Teenage Cancer Trust

"The partnership with Teenage Cancer Trust was a crucial vehicle for engaging and motivating staff and fostering employee morale during a difficult transition period for the company."

Tarun Jotwani,
Head of Global.
Nomura

"Our company now has a great deal of pride and satisfaction from being able to use our technological know-how to make a big difference to a great charity."

Darren Strowger,
Chairman.
Excell Group

FINDINGS:

Marriage – how to capture hearts and minds

The employees of both charity and corporate are the real champions of any partnership and it is their enthusiasm and creativity that delivers results. You need to make it easy for people to engage.

Inform, inspire engage: The first step in any campaign is to inform as many people as possible of the partnership aims and objectives. This initial campaign will search out natural champions and people already connected to the charity. The use of inspirational stories helps to widen the impact, preparing the way for the engagement campaign.

Making real impact: The corporate will no doubt want to demonstrate a tangible impact and successes that they can "own". It is important the charity partner can help define this and build a story that both partners are proud to tell. Recognition and strong communication are really important in driving momentum. Unique projects will emerge as you get to know each other.

Engagement: A successful partnership needs to be aware of all the ways that help drive engagement. People are all very different in what motivates them to get involved. Some prefer a passive approach and are content merely to payroll give, others will throw themselves behind ambitious fundraising activities. Others will be delighted to offer their expertise. The objective is to have a range of touch points that will appeal to different people for maximum impact.

Good partnership managers will understand all these and it is not the purpose of this guide to go into each of them in detail. The following offers a collection of ideas:

Payroll-giving: Many people hate the thought of volunteering, but will happily give a small amount on a regular basis. What is interesting about the behaviour of payroll-giving is that people rarely cancel their donation, so this particular mechanic is useful when thinking about the legacy of the partnership. Help the Hospices were the charity partner of Royal Mail Group in 2005-2007 and they still received nearly £17,000 each month from Royal Mail colleagues in 2011. It takes a sustained campaign to engage people with payroll-giving. You need an effective third-party agency and a charity partner to develop a specific campaign. It needs to be a constant feature covered in the induction literature, payroll forms and pay and bonus letters. The process needs to be easy and supported by a monthly communication plan on totals raised. This is a collective message that if everyone gave just £5 a month multiplied by the number of employees by the number of months then that equates to an incredible amount of money. Royal Mail has one of the UK's most successful payroll-giving schemes, regularly engaging 26% of the workforce and raising £2 million each year. There are awards that you can enter your company for, managed by the Institute of Fundraising, to raise the profile of your activities. On average payroll-giving contributes over £106 million to charities every year. This amount could be increased considerably if corporates raised the profile of payroll-giving and set a target to engage 25% of employees. For the corporate it provides an easy measure of engagement levels, carries a great story, is easy to deliver and has an external reward structure for PR profile – so a no-brainer to have as part of the marriage story. There was some difference amongst charities as to where payroll-giving sat – individual small donors or corporate partnerships. Often payroll-giving was missed out of the partnership approach and left instead to another part of the charity to follow up on.

Volunteering: Is a fantastic way of securing genuine understanding of each other. Volunteering does not all have to be about "done-in-a-day projects". Some charities will not be geared up for having lots of volunteers in-house but there are many ways of getting people involved. By understanding each other you will be able to identify opportunities for volunteers. Volunteering can be used to develop colleagues' skills, for team building, coaching, leadership development and life skills. Everybody has something to give, be that CV-writing skills, interview advice or just being there as someone to listen. All the evidence and research into the impact volunteering has on employee morale shows that it is a valuable training and development tool for HR. Having a main charity partnership helps to focus volunteering around a cause. Take the time to brainstorm all the ways your colleagues could help. There are some amazing emerging social enterprises that can help you design constructive volunteering programmes (see pages 103 to 107). Volunteering can also be carried out in the workplace for those businesses who find it difficult to release staff. Royal Mail operated a very successful work experience programme on-site using colleagues to mentor young people. Don't discount volunteering just because of size or location. Really explore this option.

Seeing is believing: If volunteering is not an option then explore a range of "seeing is believing" visits. These visits to see projects can be a powerful motivating experience helping to generate new ideas and inject creativity into how to help a charity partnership. Every year Tesco organises a "Seeing is Believing" visit for their directors to go and see first hand the impact that a corporate can have on a charity. Business in the Community use their "Seeing is Believing" events to engage more and more senior leaders in CR. This is a very powerful tool for engagement and nearly always sparks new ideas.

In-kind expertise: Is a great way to engage senior corporate people in the running of the charity. Deloitte made an incredible difference to Help for Heroes (chapter 8). Whizz-Kidz also benefited from the expertise of Tesco. Royal Mail delivered an award-winning direct mail campaign for Barnardo's and Nomura helped Teenage Cancer Trust when their offices were broken into. Exploring how you can share expertise can really help drive down costs and improve the efficiency of a charity's core services.

Team building: Involving cohorts of staff is sometimes a great way of creating a competitive spirit. It is a great challenge for graduates to operate as an annual cohort to be given a specific challenge. Fujitsu wanted to re-launch and reinvigorate payroll-giving and set this as a project for the graduate intake. Other organisations have used the charity partnership to organise away-days and training courses. Teenage Cancer Trust now offers management-training programmes as an innovative solution for corporate partners.

Business relationships: Supplier client engagement is also a route to explore. Why limit the relationship to your own employees and customers? Who can you target to help? Where else can you make connections?

Cause-related marketing: Can be very lucrative where a customer-facing business can engage vast numbers of customers in their CR strategy. There has been a significant rise in high-profile campaigns where business can use its communication channels to engage people. Sky and WWF have a great campaign to raise awareness of the rainforest using Sky's media voice, Sainsbury's has done an incredible job for Comic Relief and Boots' campaign on cancer awareness has been widely recognised.

Customer/client engagement: Should feature in all corporate partnership strategies. Even smaller organisations can explore how a customer engagement programme could add value. B2B companies can also engage their customers.

Fujitsu has recognised the importance of CR in its client engagement, for example, Royal Bank of Scotland is an important customer and they share a common partner with Fujitsu in The Prince's Trust, it would therefore make sense to see where they could collaborate and help team build between the two project teams. The same approach was taken between Fujitsu and HMRC using the Employers' Forum on Disability to work together on accessible IT.

Charity professionals that we spoke to also had some concerns about corporate demands for volunteering. Who is actually doing the volunteering, the individual employee or the corporate whole that releases people during paid time? Expectations that a charity could produce unique award-winning projects and celebrity guests at the drop of a hat were also a worry to some charities. In some cases charities felt more like a "supplier" than a partner. Corporates and charities will have very different values and objectives and speak different languages. These differences will need to be managed, especially if the primary purpose of a charity does not exactly fit a corporate's expectations, in order to prevent tension and misconceptions.

Conclusion: Corporates are always looking for genuine client engagement opportunities – charities can hold a unique brokerage role in this space and one that is underutilised at present. There is a plethora of ways that you can leverage a great deal of benefit from a charity-corporate partnership. What you must do is explore every touch-point and you can best do this if you know each other really well.

CASE HISTORY

Teenage Cancer Trust and Nomura Global Investment Bank

Teenage Cancer Trust know the value of spotting a good potential partner and really sticking with it to make it work. With over a third of their income generated from corporate partnerships, they appreciate the prize that can be available.

Teenage Cancer Trust (TCT) and Nomura share their experience of partnership which resulted in winning the Heart of the City Dragon Award. TCT also formed a partnership with Excell, a much smaller organisation. This case study illustrates that flexibility and the desire to really get to know your partner are the key factors to a successful relationship.

Nomura is a large global investment bank which acquired Lehman Brothers Europe and Asia businesses in 2008. This brought with it the challenge of how to integrate two organisations and create a new investment bank. There was some concern that Lehmans' tradition of substantial charitable support would end as the concept of community partnerships and employee volunteering is quite rare in Tokyo, which is Nomura's global headquarters. Despite other considerations involved in the integration, Nomura's senior management quickly realised just how important charitable partnerships were to their colleagues from Lehman Brothers and so established a dedicated function within the London office to manage these activities. A decision was made to bring in a charity partner to help unite all colleagues behind a common purpose.

Nomura was very clear on its purpose for forming a charity partnership

- To act as a clear and public display of Nomura's commitment to supporting underprivileged young people in London
- To enable all London employees to work together for a common cause
- To serve as a vehicle for engaging and motivating staff and fostering employee morale during a challenging period of business integration

TCT also had a clearly defined purpose

TCT needed a new business partner to meet an urgent need within the capital. There are an estimated 1,141 teenage and young adults in London with cancer, yet the only specialist support is just 19 beds treating 207 patients each year.

TCT had a clear understanding of its purpose. It needed a partner to

- Sponsor its flagship Albert Hall Tenth Anniversary concert series
- Expand its service provision to young people fighting cancer
- Build eight treatment pods at the Day Care Centre at University College London Hospital
- Raise awareness of the issues affecting young people with cancer

The Dating Game was taken very seriously by Nomura with the Community Affairs team interviewing over thirty charities and then asking colleagues to vote from a preferred short list of six. TCT pitched for the staff vote and over 1,000 (25%) employees voted.

TOP TIP: "Build relationships between senior management and key contacts at all levels across both organisations. This includes inviting influential stakeholders to see the work of the charity through attending events organised by the charity. This will enable the charity to receive support from the top down and engage employees across the organisation."

Anthony Harte,
Head of Community Affairs.
EMEA Nomura

TCT was the clear winner. A contract was drawn up with a joint aspiration and this two-year partnership was agreed to run from May 2009 to April 2011. A goal of £100,000 was set as a fundraising target.

TCT wanted to understand the needs and culture of Nomura, enabling it to tailor the fundraising and engagement accordingly, so Nomura took an innovative approach to building the partnership. Nomura agreed to provide TCT with access to all of Nomura's resources to support the partnership.

Nomura created an open-door policy, so that TCT representatives could talk to the senior executive team whenever they wanted – and vice versa. This relationship extended to the two CEOs. Nomura's Community Affairs team also spent a day every quarter brainstorming volunteering and charity activities for TCT at the charity's offices. Communication was an essential component of the relationship, with a dedicated intranet site showcasing progress and sharing what was happening to inspire more engagement amongst staff.

Within 20 months Nomura had surpassed its goal of £100,000 and had raised a staggering £1 million. These funds enabled TCT to double its reach in treating young people diagnosed with cancer in London.

In addition to direct income, the partnership has other wide-reaching benefits for TCT:

- When TCT recently needed to expand their offices, Nomura donated furniture from its own office, saving TCT £10,000.
- When the charity had a break-in, Nomura provided security expertise to advise on future security measures.
- The charity has been able to engage with other potential corporate funders thanks to direct introductions from Nomura. These included construction firm Bancroft, which recently chose TCT as its "Charity of the Year", and has already raised £40,000.
- Nomura provides facilities for TCT's events and annual strategy days.

The partnership with TCT gave employees something positive to unite them and make them feel proud of working at Nomura. A December 2010 employee survey revealed that:

- 96% of employees are aware of the partnership – this is a great result that all charity partnerships should aspire to achieve.
- The 65% of employees who said they were very familiar with the TCT partnership display on average 38% more pride at working for Nomura than those who are not aware of the link.

The partnership also brought a positive image to Nomura at a key time when there was a negative opinion of the City: The concert at the Albert Hall alone generated newspaper/magazine coverage valued at £31,646 and TV coverage valued at £50,000.

CASE HISTORY

Excell Group Ltd and TCT

The association with Excell Group and TCT began very differently to TCT's partnership with Nomura. By way of an introduction between the two CEOs a courtship emerged and a relationship blossomed. The Excell Group now has a long-standing association with TCT, which continues to go from strength to strength. For Excell Group it was never about raising vast sums of money or staff engagement but looking at what they could do for TCT using their expertise.

The relationship grew from recognition that internet-based technologies would enable secure, person-to-person communication, which is simple yet far reaching and would have a practical and financial benefit to TCT.

It has been a logical progression for Excell to be engaged at the cutting edge of delivery of systems, services and applications to support the charity's efforts to help teenage cancer patients and reduce telephone costs at the same time. The foundations were laid with the delivery and installation of an Avaya IP Office telephony system, complete with VoiceMail Pro in the TCT's Newman Street head office in London. This small but powerful IP PBX has enabled TCT to streamline their company communications and save money on calls and line rental. The VoiceMail application has provided a frontline means to route calls to the correct destination while allowing for voice messages to be left in the absence of the intended party.

Darren Strowger, Excell Chairman and TCT Patron commented, "Teenage Cancer Trust is a fantastic charity striving to make life better for these young people. As a parent myself, I feel it's important that we recognise that teenagers have different needs from children and adults, and to that end it's important that we do what we can to help. Creating awareness of TCT and the fact that the specialist needs of these teenagers are not currently recognised within the NHS system is an ongoing challenge and Excell strives to promote the remarkable work being done by TCT."

Delivering head office technology was only the starting point for Excell in providing more support to young adult cancer patients, equivalent Avaya IP Office systems were installed in the TCT units in Manchester and Leeds. As further new units opened, networking them together to support a broad range of internet based applications became of strategic importance to TCT. The next step for Excell is to provide voice and data solutions at new units in Sheffield, Birmingham, Newcastle, Liverpool and Addenbrooks Hospital in Cambridge.

Putting teenagers in touch with other teenagers has been identified as one of the strongest methods to assist in remission. For the patients, it means that they can do so for virtually unlimited time with other patients across the UK at no cost, sharing their experiences and advice on coping with cancer.

Excell are introducing further cost-saving applications to each participating unit. The need for teenagers to feel included and supported will shortly be extended to allow for videoconferencing between units with the internet as the connection media. This allows doctors, nurses and oncologist consultants to hold patient review sessions "on-line", saving time while exchanging information and data in real time.

The partnership with Excell Group was based on using their expertise and technological know-how, combined with a passion to get involved to make a real difference to the operations of TCT. The result reduced costs and improved the experience of patients.

TOP TIP: "A partnership is not always about targeting a lot of staff to raise funds. A strategic alliance can deliver huge benefits if you can spot the synergy and opportunity. Smaller businesses have a great deal to offer if approached in the right way."

Darren Strowger,
Chairman.
Excell Group

ACTION POINT 6:

Explore every option at your disposal to get the best from each other. Tried and tested formulas work well but innovative and exciting approaches really test each partner's skill and ability.

Marriage – Engage hearts and minds

Partnerships are ultimately about people. The objectives of all partnerships are about motivating and inspiring people so that they can make a significant and lasting contribution. Action Point 6 is all about creating a communication and engagement process that can tell a powerful story that captures people's imagination.

Both partners must ensure that the hygiene factors are all in place such as payroll-giving schemes, volunteering policies, matched funding etc. People will be put off by complicated processes. Make engagement simple and effective.

Ensure the right combination of talent and personalities are in place to deliver success on a daily basis. Feedback from the corporate sector was a plea not to put an inexperienced fundraiser in charge of a corporate partnership. It was clear that the general belief was that the partnership director should be capable of understanding a much wider remit than just fundraising. Equally, charities that are very experienced at running partnerships did not want to be contained within a CR department but be given access to all areas of a corporate.

Ensure a structure is put in place that promotes the effective delivery of the partnership. Success comes when a wide engagement is secured across both organisations. Creating silos for a partnership, restricting access and being too prescriptive will stifle engagement and creativity.

Create the right circumstances that allow people to generate innovative ideas and find new ways of working.

In 2010, 271 charities were supported by employees of the Bibby Line Group with £880,000 raised through a combination of employee fundraising and giving and company match-funding. This was the result of a programme designed to encourage employee participation. Eighty-five per cent of the company's 4,100 workforce is engaged in volunteering, fundraising or payroll-giving. The Giving Something Back programme is integrated into how the group does business. Employees are not told what to fundraise for, but are encouraged to support charities that are important to them personally. The company ensures that it can support its employees by having a range of processes in place to support payroll-giving, fundraising and volunteering.

SECRETS TO SUCCESS

The ups and downs – keep talking

Success comes from passion and commitment – you need to create the right environment to allow the relationship to flourish.

Exercise:

How will you engage people at all levels? In chapter 5 the authors explored the vital element of leadership. You need to develop a clear strategy for extending this engagement right across both organisations.

How will you ensure open communication? Nomura had an innovative solution of embedding a key member of the TCT staff within its own organisation. Royal Mail Group created a monthly partnership board. Deloitte had key senior personnel driving the partnership forward. What you must do is establish a powerful mechanic for ensuring speedy and honest communications. This is the key learning from all the case studies in this guide. Success comes from the closeness of the two organisations. Make sure when working through Action Points 3 and 4 you establish the right structure for your communication strategy. Revisit Action Point 6 regularly to make sure it is working.

Have you recruited the right talent to manage the partnership? Stability and consistency are important. Nomura felt strongly that if possible one person from TCT should be embedded in their organisation for the two years. Choosing the right person that could be trusted to deliver was important. Deloitte also emphasised the need for a lead person from the charity. Douglas Campbell-Rouse also made this point in his expert commentary in chapter 2. It takes a certain kind of skill set to work closely with a corporate culture. Charities need to invest in recruiting and retaining good people. A comment shared from several corporates was that much of the charities' effort was directed to winning the pitch and not in managing the partnership. An innovative approach is to ask the corporate to second a person to the charity for the duration of the partnership.

Have you explored all the delivery mechanics? There are many different delivery ideas. You need to set aside time to understand where all your touch points are. Brainstorm all the areas in which you could create value.

Have you a process for recording your journey? In chapter 8 we explore recognition and reward. Being able to tell a compelling story will win you coveted awards. Don't underestimate how hard it is to recall every step in your partnership journey. At Royal Mail the three-year journey with Barnardo's was extremely busy and at the end of the partnership it was not that easy to recall all the successes and all the pitfalls. In chapter 10 we discuss the importance of reflections and producing a lessons learned paper. Think about the process now – can you build a blog and an online diary? Keep all your press cuttings and collect the evidence for your case study as you go along.

SIMON DAVIES

Chief Executive Officer of TCT shares his views of what makes a successful partnership

"A charity-corporate partnership is one of the best ways to raise revenue and give you access to large numbers of people to grow your contact database. You need to be prepared to offer a highly professional approach and be prepared to invest a great deal of time and energy into the relationship, if you do the rewards can be great.

A great relationship manager from both the corporate and charity perspective is essential. From the charity side having an 'access all areas' pass is something we try and negotiate, it makes all the difference to how you work together. A failing on the side of some corporates is that they sideline the charity relationship into the CR department. In my view this approach can cause problems. Integration is critical.

TCT follows the principle that embedding the relationship manager into the corporate partner is important for several reasons. It really helps you get under the skin of the corporate and understand their culture and move effortlessly through the corporate. Having a desk and an internal phone number, even if this is just one day a week, means that our relationship manager is treated more like a fellow colleague of the corporate. This does of course mean you have to choose your relationship managers with care – you need to be able to trust their professionalism and ability to deal with a corporate culture. What this gives you is the ability to recognise the different approaches taken by internal teams. For example, at Nomura the sales team on the trading floor were really competitive but the catering colleagues were not so, it was all about 'horses for courses'.

When we partnered with Nomura we knew from the beginning that employee engagement was their driver for wanting a charity partner. We worked together on building an award-winning engagement strategy developing training tools and a variety of projects.

I have never agreed with the position of the 'cap-in-hand' charity approach that we are a worthy cause. TCT always takes the view of a shared aim with a joint benefit whenever we approach a relationship. Of course the objective is to raise funds, but this must sit within a wider framework of benefits. It's about believing in the philosophy of engagement. Fun is another big component – the whole point to feel good about these partnerships and get people involved. We always make sure we ask for regular feedback from colleagues and stay in tune with their experience.

Our relationship with Excell Group is very different from Nomura. At the beginning we were less clear on what we would eventually achieve together but we spotted that Excell Chairman Darren Strowger was an extremely committed individual and we recognised the potential of the relationship. We just kept exploring avenues and we grew together, now we have an amazing relationship with them."

TOP TIP: "You must invest time and effort in all your relationships to get results. Charities must be flexible and capable of recognising a whole range of partnership styles and opportunities. Get up close and personal to your partner and think of the benefits to both parties when looking to raise funds."

SUMMARY

Managing the ups and downs

Having a powerful engagement strategy which can reach out to all potential stakeholders and touch-points of both partners is what will really deliver amazing results. There will be challenges in bringing together different cultures and values into a partnership; you will need to work hard to overcome barriers and problems.

An engagement strategy will:

- Create fertile ground to generate creative ideas
- Reveal natural champions for the charity cause
- Achieve the widest possible reach for the charity partner
- Help overcome barriers/bottlenecks
- Open up potential new contact points

Think about:

- Embedding the relationship managers in each other's organisations
- Having an 'access all areas' pass
- The corporate seconding the relationship manager to the charity
- Sharing the journey as it unfolds with all colleagues
- Capturing every moment of the relationship.

TEN-POINT ACTION PLAN		
Action Point 1	Single	Know your purpose
Action Point 2	Dating	Create a compelling proposal
Action Point 3	Engaged	Agree a joint strategy
Action Point 4	Vows	Draw up a written agreement
Action Point 5	Honeymoon	Secure top-level commitment
Action Point 6	**Marriage**	**Engage hearts and minds ✓**

CHAPTER SEVEN

The benefits

JOINT ACCOUNT? – OR SEPARATE INCOMES?

HOW WILL YOU THE VALUE THE BENEFITS OF YOUR PARTNERSHIP?

The value of a partnership is not just about how much the corporate partner can raise in cash, or offer in-kind services for the charity. It is about understanding the needs and expectations of both partners, and making sure that you bring all the relevant assets from your organisations to the table.

Your understanding of the value of your partnership will help leverage maximum benefit.

"We believe our relationship with the Bromley by Bow Centre is an excellent example of how businesses can integrate CR principles within their core business activities, allowing us to build solid financial performance while also making a positive contribution to the wider community and environment in which we operate."

David Taylor-Smith,
Chief Executive.
G4S Secure Solutions

"It has always been clear to me that the key to our relationship with G4S is shared values. We are both committed to excellence and providing the most coherent and effective solutions as possible. Essentially we are both running organisations (albeit on very different scales) which are about valuing people and delivering high quality services. Our relationship with G4S is about finding areas of mutuality that can add real value to both of our businesses."

Rob Trimble,
Chief Executive.
Bromley by Bow Centre

FINDINGS:

The benefits – how to value each other

The true value of the partnership can be measured across a wide range of issues. It is no longer a one-way stream of value, from corporate to charity. It is a two-way process with expectations of mutual benefits and value creation individually as well as jointly. The challenge is how to value all the benefits alongside the actual cash generated.

Changing roles: In traditional partnerships, the corporate partner often has the role of the donor and contributor and the charity is seen as the recipient and beneficiary. The benefits derived from a partnership are in the main described as benefits to the charity, its cause and end-users. However, the donor/beneficiary relationship has been replaced by many different complex forms of relations, where the partners take turns in being suppliers, business managers, donors, lobbyists, customers etc. There is value in exploring how these differing roles add value to the partnership.

New economic environment: There is an emerging new demand for cross-sector partnerships, coalitions and consortia, which requires evidence of partner credentials. Partnership working has become mandatory in some cases, not just voluntary and philanthropic, and many organisations are struggling to make this difficult art work for them.

Value creation: The appreciation and understanding of the economic value of a partnership increases over time as trust, honesty and knowledge of each other become stronger. As the relationship matures, greater exploration of added value becomes more meaningful.

Help for Heroes identified that they could provide Deloitte with publicity and exposure to a non-business audience through its flagship concert event, an innovation for Deloitte that mainly works business to business.

Camfed realised that beyond Linklaters' corporate support to developing the charity's governance, using the findings more generally in a public report would help Linklaters carve out a strategic position for the company regarding governance expertise and debate.

Efficiency savings: Many partnerships start with an initial focus of supporting a charity's frontline delivery, but in time turn to focus on internal and often mutually beneficial capacity building. As regards the the economy of the partnership, the greatest value in the corporate/charity partnership often lies in strengthening back office capacity and efficiency of operations and sharing organisational learning and solutions from both organisations.

Innovation: For companies, choosing a charity partner where they can create real and visible impact is important. Where previously large and well-known charities were the partners of choice, the trend is for corporates to partner with smaller, less well-known organisations with the intention of growing the charity and changing its profile. Companies are looking for opportunities of leaving the legacy of a transformed and strengthened charity as a result of the partnership.

G4S, the UK's leading provider of custodial services, and St Giles Trust, a prominent UK charity which supports ex-offenders, have formed a strategic partnership aimed at tackling reoffending rates and improving the rehabilitation of offenders.

Route to market: All charities face the challenge of getting their message out to their target audience in an environment that is crowded with social action. Being able to use an existing route to market can save millions in advertising and deliver a more targeted campaign message.

The Prostate Cancer Charity has partnered with LoveFilm. The partnership has deliberately not set fundraising targets as this is unexplored territory for the men's health charity. The challenge is that prostate cancer is seen as an old man's disease, and taking this message to a younger audience has always been difficult. LoveFilm has 40% of the DVD rental market and is using its online presence to create innovate campaigns, including the use of film to raise awareness of prostate cancer with young men.

Access to volunteers: Many corporates recognise the value in supporting volunteering and some have a formal release policy. Charities can access vast numbers of people in ways they need support, both from a specific talent perspective to more general assistance. This area is still evolving and discovering how best to match charities with people.

Homebase launched a volunteering policy in January 2011 providing opportunities for all colleagues to spend two days per year making a difference in their local community. It has been widely used to support team building and colleagues' own personal development.

Conclusion: There is no doubt that when a charity partners with a corporate, there is the potential to make a massive difference to the cause being championed. This kind of collaboration definitely results in the sum of the parts being greater than the whole. The unique value that each partner brings has the capacity to grow the ability of both partners.

CASE HISTORY

G4S and Bromley by Bow Centre discuss joining forces for mutual development

G4S is the largest security services company in the UK and Ireland with a turnover of more than £1.2 billion and 40,000 employees. More than 6,000 customers, including the majority of UK Government departments and many schools and community health centres, depend on G4S to provide them with a safe and secure way to deliver their services.

Bromley by Bow Centre (BbBC) is an innovative health centre in the East End of London with around 100 staff. They use a radical approach to delivering primary care and opened the first health centre in Britain that was owned by the patients and rented back to the GPs. In addition, BbBC offers its patients a range of on-site services including work on allotments, vocational training courses, English lessons and a BA degree in social enterprise.

In response to government Private Finance Initiatives (PFI) in 2002, G4S took a business decision to develop their approach to the building and managing of health centres. G4S identified the need for a partner with experience in healthcare who could help position their brand as a leader in this area. BbBC matched these needs.

G4S and Bromley by Bow Centre developed a unique partnership model that involves the BbBC, a charity, providing business development support to a private sector organisation, G4S. The partnership has resulted in a reciprocal business relationship that benefits both organisations.

Working in partnership with BbBC, G4S was awarded the government's first ever Local Improvement Finance Trust (LIFT) contract which has led to the building of seven new health centres in East London. BbBC has provided basic skills training for G4S ancillary staff at the Mile End Hospital site, and BbBC's landscaping social enterprise provides grounds maintenance to 26 schools in Tower Hamlets, appointed through G4S's PFI contract. More recently, BbBC developed a job brokerage scheme for G4S to support its work on the Olympic site in East London. In return, BbBC has received expert support from G4S on facilities management, human resources, communications, risk management and strategic business development. Recently, a G4S senior director joined the BbBC's board.

TOP TIP: "The true value of a partnership lies in the mutual benefit and added value that each partner gains. Innovative solutions emerge when two very different organisations work together."

Rob Trimble,
Chief Executive.
Bromley by Bow Centre

ACTION POINT 7:

A partnership can add capacity that enables both partners to grow and develop services strategically. Innovative partnerships can offer a unique set of benefits which are about forming a core relationship and doing business together.

Benefits – Negotiate mutually beneficial terms

As a relationship matures new opportunities will emerge. Understanding the different types of benefit throughout the collaboration will help make the partnership fit for purpose. It is important to explore constantly all the areas where value can be added.

Value creation takes on many forms from cost efficiency, skill transfer, capacity building to access to new networks and routes to market. Refer back to the core purpose of the partnership to ensure that everything is being done to deliver the main objectives.

It is important to recognise that the flow of benefit is not always one way. Typically, it could be assumed that the charity will be main beneficiary. However, in some cases the corporate partner will be the main beneficiary as the charity invests time and money in providing a service, such as training, volunteering opportunities or events management.

For these reasons it is important to be able to define all the potential benefits and understand exactly what constitutes value for your partner. As you get to know each other better you will each gain a better sense of the available opportunities.

It is important to measure the value of the partnership and demonstrate the impact in all the areas of work, not just fundraising totals.

Establishing mutual capacity building and playing to the strength of each organisation is a key factor in managing the economy of the partnership. It is cost efficient, more comfortable and much less frustrating for partners to do what they are good at and contribute key resources to the partnership.

Samaritans and Network Rail joined forces to tackle the high number of suicides on railways. The partnership, over five years, will be delivered through training for all rail staff in dealing with potential suicides and the aftermath of suicide. The high loss of life is clearly a tragedy and something that needs to be tackled. In addition, each year suicides cost the train operators around £15 million. By working together this innovative partnership aims to reduce the number of suicides on the railways by 20%.

SECRETS TO SUCCESS

Reciprocity – two-way street

The objective is to achieve a high value sustainable partnership that is mutually beneficial. The key is to know what constitutes value for you and your partner, and how you can both contribute and receive most value and the best joint results from the partnership.

Exercise:

What role does each partner play? To match contributions and different forms of investments from both sides of the table, you should identify together the different types of roles you are playing in the relationship. Be aware that these roles may change as the relationship develops.

What contributions are most suited to your partner? Your choice of contribution should be guided by what you both want to get out of the partnership. The joint strategy will identify goals, you need to explore how best to work together in order to achieve them.

Are your contributions creating a lasting change? If the charity partner wants long-term financial stability and development, then the support to developing business opportunities and support systems may be a better contribution than a large sum of restricted funding. Partnerships are best and most successful when they instigate/provide change in both organisations.

Frontline support or behind-the-scenes capacity? Discuss with your partner whether your partnership should mainly focus on activities behind the scenes, to support and build organisational capacity and efficiency or aim at frontline work with end-users and beneficiaries. This is also a very important point when you consider how to deploy volunteers to support the partnership.

Do you know who the most valuable stakeholders are? The corporate partners should consider whether, for example, employee engagement or investor relations are more important and the charity should direct its efforts to achieve this goal. The charity should consider whether, for example, policy influence or improved delivery connections take priority and discuss this with the corporate partner.

How will you measure the value of the partnership? At this stage, start conversations with your partner on how you individually and jointly measure the value of input and outcomes of the partnership. Do you have the same or different criteria, and will you set up a joint framework to capture progress?

MARTIN JOHNSTON & STEVE MOORE

Co-Founders of Brandanomics discuss the benefits of the corporate charity partnership

"There is, and to a certain extent always has been, a view that businesses and charities are mutually exclusive, that profit and philanthropy rarely go hand in hand. It is hardly surprising then that when corporates 'do charity' it is regarded with barely concealed cynicism. Part of the problem lies with CR that is all too often an ineffectual bolt-on that means little more than ticking a box in the annual report. If CR departments are to be more than the modern-day equivalent of a collecting tin on reception, then both companies and charities need to understand the mutual benefits of shared skills, services and ideals.

Charities need to recognise how they can benefit from brand association, reputation, reach and logistic capabilities of business which means realising that an increasing number of global companies see social impact as an integral part of their business operation. Equally, the corporate sector must acknowledge the expertise, commitment and ability to achieve much on limited resources that charities understand.

Charities and businesses may superficially have very different aims but in fact, share a great deal – not least of all surviving and maximising their income during these tough economic times and using their resources wisely. When they work together, intertwine their shared purposes and commit to a wider social impact for the common good, they will achieve far more.

There are numerous examples of partnerships that have arguably been far more effective because of such a relationship, Sainsbury's support for Comic Relief, Starbucks' commitment to Fair Trade products and Deloitte's support for Help for Heroes are but a handful, and there are many more.

That is why social impact can only truly be delivered when CR is more than fundraising – when it becomes part of a company's DNA and thus, an integral part of their brand reputation. Presenting a substantial cheque to a good cause is diminished in real, lasting value if the donor does not appear to empathise with the cause it's supporting, whether it's sustainability, ethical investment or working with the wider community. Welcome as any charitable donation may be, it has much more impact on the perception of a brand if it is based on common values, a commitment to 'giving' more than money: maybe expertise, mentoring or pro bono services.

Increasingly, shareholders, clients and potential investors look beyond a company's accounts to assess its core values, and for demonstrable evidence of its commitment to the wider community; similarly, charities that are seen to be supported by trusted brands will benefit hugely. Together really is stronger."

TOP TIP: "Collaboration is key to a successful co-existence. The potential from working together is enormous in terms of accelerating social impact and influence for both charities and business."

SUMMARY

The added benefits of marriage

Understanding the benefits and value that a partnership could deliver will help you push the boundaries of your expectations, receiving even greater rewards.

Negotiate mutually beneficial terms:

- Financial contributions
- In-kind donations
- Commercial initiatives
- Pro bono services
- Volunteering

Be innovative in looking at:

- Communications – visibility, new audiences
- Access to new markets – supply chain and consumer engagement
- Extended reputational reach – influencing wider public policy
- Capitalising on the uniqueness of the partnership
- Leveraging the trust in both brands

TEN-POINT ACTION PLAN		
Action Point 1	Single	Know your purpose
Action Point 2	Dating	Create a compelling proposal
Action Point 3	Engaged	Agree a joint strategy
Action Point 4	Vows	Draw up a written agreement
Action Point 5	Honeymoon	Secure top-level commitment
Action Point 6	Marriage	Engage hearts and minds
Action Point 7	**Benefits**	**Negotiate mutually beneficial terms** ✓

CHAPTER EIGHT

Date nights

HOW DO YOU KNOW THE MARRIAGE IS WORKING?

HOW DO YOU KEEP THE ROMANCE ALIVE?

Great partnerships thrive on passion and excitement.

Action Point 8 explores how to keep the momentum in a long-term partnership, how to recognise impact and celebrate success.

"Deloitte has become integral to our business strategy. They are part of the team. I can get sophisticated help to tackle long-term issues as we grow our charity."

Bryn Parry,
CEO.
Help for Heroes

"By getting under the skin of how and why a company wants to support the community, the third sector stands to benefit more, for longer, from a genuine partnership with business."

Heather Hancock,
Managing Partner for Innovation.
Deloitte

FINDINGS:

Date nights – using your progress to re-engage

The engagement strategy launched in Action Point 6 will have created an initial wave of enthusiasm. The challenge is to sustain engagement, target new audiences and reinvigorate the campaign messages throughout the duration of the partnership. There are a range of techniques used by successful partnerships to sustain a long-term relationship. These techniques usually centre on measuring progress, reporting success and the celebration of achievements.

Measuring progress: Regular monitoring and evaluation helps keep the focus on progress. Successful partnerships use the monitoring cycle to schedule milestones in their work together, and they actively use the information to celebrate progress and excite internal and external audiences about the success to date. This technique is also useful for gauging the effectiveness of the overall campaign. Measures such as payroll-giving uptake, numbers of volunteers, consumer engagement etc. are all useful underlying indicators of steady progress. It is really helpful to be able to use measurable indicators when reporting a story.

Reporting success: Regular use of impact stories keeps people engaged and reinforces the campaign purpose. A strong communication strategy will have a sustainable message that can be refreshed periodically. Personal stories and illustrations bring a project alive. Use of community boards, newsletters and websites are all useful mechanics for keeping people up to date. There is a balance between reporting on the bigger picture and measureable success and keeping it personal and real.

In 2010/11 over 600,000 Macmillan cancer information leaflets and 35 million dispensing bags with Macmillan information were distributed to all Boots UK stores. Nationally over 3,600 pharmacists were trained in cancer awareness. Over 6,000 colleagues engaged in 'Miles for Macmillan'. The first year of the partnership raised £2.5 million. All 620 new trainees got involved in local healthcare projects. Boots No7 make-up consultants ran free sessions on skin care. By the end of 2010/11 workshops were taking place in 60 hospitals with over 120 consultants involved.

Indicators of success: Many organisations are wary about spending too much time and resources on measurement, rather than on the cause and common objectives themselves. With much ongoing debate on impact measurement, some warn about the tendency to "measure for measurement sake". A guiding principle is to limit your selection of indicators of success to those that firstly will enable you to communicate your story of progress and results, and secondly will inform you of the effectiveness of the partnership and enable you to make improvements. Success stories are within themselves incredibly motivating.

Transparency: Honesty and transparency when communicating results will enhance the credibility of a partnership with its stakeholders. Many partnerships find it difficult to make targets publicly available, in fear of the scrutiny and consequences if targets are not achieved. Sensitivity around financial reporting is vital, as any fundraising, no matter how small, is still a great achievement. Missing a financial target could be viewed negatively. It is better to set broad aims and aspirations for communication purposes to motivate people to achieve more.

Date nights: Successful partnerships build in mechanisms to generate new ideas and innovative solutions. The monitoring cycle can help create the right environment to have inspiring dialogue, spark new ideas and cement the relationship over and above the daily running of things.

Refreshing the message: Some organisations, mainly corporates, experience message fatigue, especially with their internal audiences, and the inclination is often "do something new" or "start something new" to reignite interest. Using the message of progress, improvement and changes to a long-term partnership can be equally, if not more, powerful engaging people, and the monitoring of a partnership can provide the new stories and innovation to keep the message fresh.

Asda has been incredibly successful in keeping the Tickled Pink campaign refreshed every year. Now in its fifteenth year the campaign benefits two cancer charities – Breast Cancer Care and Breast Cancer Campaign. Since it started it has raised over £25 million. The campaign constantly launches new products and activities which are clearly communicated on the Asda charity website.

Brand reputation: Reputation and credibility are core drivers for companies as the CR agenda is pushed further up the corporate business agenda. All the contributors from the corporate sector believe the charity-corporate partnership is becoming a strategic issue with clear expectations of success. Companies are always looking for ways to assess how their brand is perceived. Charities can often provide new and innovative ideas to measure brand reputation, especially in the current financial situation – reputation has to be earned.

Efficiency savings: Strong processes for review generate new solutions to increasing efficiency, reducing costs and improving the service delivery for the charity partner. As the corporate partner gets to know the charity partner well, new areas where expertise can be offered emerge, as we saw with Teenage Cancer Trust, Whizz-Kidz, Help for Heroes and Camfed. It is important to capture the value added from efficiency savings.

External recognition: There are a lot of prestigious awards for which you can enter a partnership. Winning an award can often provide a real boost for the corporate teams. Save the Children have introduced their own awards to recognise their corporate partners. Many corporates have internal recognition awards. The charity partnership is often a great way to identify community champions and give the partnership a boost.

In a tribute to how well the partnership developed, Save the Children recognised Reckitt Benckiser with an award at their first corporate award ceremony. Sandra Hennessy, Global Corporate Communications & Affairs Manager at RB, also won an award for the most outstanding individual and said, "I was more than a little shocked, but hugely proud, to receive this award. I am proud of the passion and commitment of my colleagues around the world, whose efforts are improving the lives of children."

Conclusion: Successful partnerships are capable of distilling their joint success into clear measurable impact statements that are readily understood by a range of audiences. Success generates success as people feel proud to be associated with a partnership that is making a real difference. This ability to show demonstrable impact also helps secure that award-winning proposal.

CASE HISTORY

Deloitte and Help for Heroes on making a marriage work well

Deloitte is one of the UK's leading business advisory firms with thousands of dedicated professionals who provide audit, consulting, financial advisory, risk management, and tax services to selected clients. Deloitte has a long history of support for the wider community.

Help for Heroes supports those who have been wounded in Britain's current conflicts. Founded in October 2007 by Bryn and Emma Parry, the original goal was to raise £10,000 following a profoundly moving visit to Selly Oak Hospital in the summer of 2007. It is now one of the most recognised brands in the UK and has grown to raise more than £120 million. A key part of its activity is the development of personnel recovery centres for wounded ex-servicemen and women, providing both practical and emotional support and a full range of services, such as skills training, career advice, emotional support and physical rehabilitation – all of which help people in their journey from the armed forces back into civilian life or, where possible, back into active service.

Deloitte and Help for Heroes started their partnership in early 2010 as a standard "Charity of the Year" relationship. Help for Heroes were honest to Deloitte about their lack of experience with corporate engagement and their expectations of the partnership were predicated on a fundraising model only. Relationships were developed at senior levels and throughout both organisations. This resulted in lots of early discussions that enabled the two organisations to get to know each other.

Deloitte quickly recognised the pressure that rapid growth was having on the charity. Within three years of starting, the charity was in excess of seeing a turnover of £40 million which was creating huge amounts of strain on the organisation. Having not really adapted or changed its structure since it was founded, it now was struggling to cope effectively with the number of new opportunities that were developing.

The lead relationship partner for Deloitte, Tony Schofield, realised that Help for Heroes' situation was much akin to that of a small business in super growth – an area where Deloitte offers professional services. He started to understand the charity in more detail, its strategy and plans to grow, and the partnership quickly moved from one focused on pure fundraising to one including organisational development. And so a journey began that leveraged high-level management support from Deloitte on a pro bono basis. Accessing professional expertise and people-resource to develop and strengthen Help for Heroes' infrastructure and governance enabled the charity to cope with its immense success and rapid growth.

Deloitte provided Help for Heroes with an overall organisational structure review, an IT systems review, property consultancy and significant implementation support by seconding their professional staff to Help for Heroes and giving broader access to Deloitte experts. Where Deloitte did not have the expertise in-house, the firm introduced technical partners to the partnership. These organisations subsequently provided their own pro bono support and much more. This way, Deloitte has helped to introduce new contacts some of which have developed into real long-term partnerships.

One of the key benefits to stem from the partnership was leadership support. Tony Schofield provided personal support to the CEO Bryn Parry, when it was clear that the passion and enthusiasm that originally drove the development of the charity wasn't enough on its own anymore to lead a big operation with multiple projects.

The charity also benefited from a look at the organisation through a corporate lens. Although Help for Heroes is a pioneering and innovative organisation, it could never get ahead in its planning and was always chasing and catching up. They needed help to get ahead.

With each solution provided, Deloitte was very mindful not to create dependencies and only suggested solutions that the charity could manage itself. As an example, an interim Head of IT was seconded from Deloitte to help build capacity and subsequently create a permanent solution and recruit the right person to Help for Heroes.

TOP TIP: "There is great appeal in wanting to be able to have real impact in areas where you can make a material change. Charities should have an open mind and be ready to explore how truly to work together."
Tony Schofield,
Partner.
Deloitte

From the Deloitte side, the benefits of this level of engagement were significant. Its integral association with the success of such a high-profile charity provided an unprecedented opportunity to engage and develop its staff, strengthen client relationships and showcase its core business capabilities. It has also fundamentally changed the way in which the firm approaches its community partnerships. The approach is now based on much longer three-year partnerships, with robust governance structures from senior level down and a real focus on how the core skills and expertise of the firm can be leveraged to solve key strategic issues facing its partners.

ACTION POINT 8:

A regular monitoring cycle helps to keep the focus on progress. Underlying statistics (payroll-giving, volunteering etc) reflect the trend of overall engagement. Reporting success and celebrating achievements helps keep people enthusiastic.

Date Nights – Celebrate and recognise success
When a partnership is launched, identify expected progress and success indicators. Keep track of these indicators on a regular basis. Underlying trends are a good indication of general progress.

Decide what to measure and track regular progress. These measures should not be confined to fundraising but where possible the partnership should aim to "monetise" efficiency savings and benefit delivery.

Report success against the key measures to all the stakeholders. Reporting can range from top-line achievements to individual impact stories. It is important to tailor reporting to the audience in order to generate the right level of engagement.

Celebrate the success and effectiveness of the partnership. External recognition, press reporting and awards reinforce the value of the partnership.

Celebrate the wider benefits of the partnership not just the results it is creating. It is important to explore how each partner values the partnership approach and how preferable it is to being single.

Partnerships that are honest about what went wrong as well as what went right will increase their credibility with both internal and external audiences. This transparency will also allow partnerships to showcase how they have made improvements and their experience may be used to educate other organisations in their approach to partnerships.

Respect in a partnership will also arise from the courage to address critical or controversial issues with the partner. Repeated best practice can become boring and idle, and claims to be perfect will not help the partnership to progress. Some charities tackle really deep-rooted problems in society that would benefit from a corporate partnership. Experienced corporates should embrace more challenging collaborations.

Afrikids, with Ghana Health Service and Southampton University Hospitals (the GAS Partnership) won the Third Sector excellence awards in 2011 for the best Public Sector Partnership. This partnership has clear objectives and can measure the impact it has by the training delivered to colleagues in Ghana, equipment delivered and funds raised. Recognition is a testament to the commitment of everyone involved.

SECRETS TO SUCCESS

Sustaining the romance – remember the anniversaries

John Gray gives the following advice to couples: "Through understanding the hidden difference of the opposite sex we can more successfully give and receive the love that is in our hearts. By validating and accepting our differences, creative solutions can be discovered."

Exercise:

Do you have a monitoring process in place? Develop a monitoring cycle that makes sense for both organisations and will allow you to use the information to make useful changes to the partnership. Give yourself time to reflect on the efficiency of the partnership and use this opportunity to connect with your partner. Monthly reviews should happen with the operational teams, while quarterly reviews should be in place for executive and strategic reviews.

Do you have the right measure of success? Make sure that you carefully select a limited number of indicators of success that are measurable and will reflect the benefits to the charity, the benefits to the company, as well as the progress on the common objectives.

- The guide More than Making Money[8] provides good advice on developing measurement.
- The LBG model[9] provides an approach to measure a company's overall contribution to the community.

Monthly figures can be tracked that give a sense of general progress, including payroll-giving levels, fundraising, volunteering etc.

How will you report results? There will be multiple audiences to a partnership and its progress, and it is worth considering how different forms of reporting will address different types of stakeholders. Means of reporting include websites, reports, newsletters, webinars, debates and consultations etc. Reporting can begin from the very start of a partnership by publishing the objectives and targets. This should be followed by progress reports on results and developments.

Remember to tell your story: Telling a story of the journey of a partnership is a powerful way to demonstrate why the partnership formed, the ambitions hoped for and how success was delivered. Case studies help bring press releases to life and aid learning. Case studies and evidence can also help you to win prestigious awards, and awards are a great way to show that a third party recognises your work and is willing to help communicate your success.

Be ready to change: Partnerships will evolve over time and the roles and relations will change. Make sure that you are ready to change, and use the evidence of measurement and progress to convey your improvements and changes to the partnership.

[8] http://www.bitc.org.uk/resources/publications/more_than_making.html
[9] http://www.lbg-online.net/about-lbg/the-lbg-model.aspx

CAMPBELL ROBB

Chief Executive Officer at Shelter gives his point of view

"Shelter's mission is to enable everyone to access, keep and retain a home in which they can thrive. As housing need increases and external funding lessens, sophisticated commercial partnerships will play an increasingly vital and varied role in enabling Shelter to achieve its goal, for example:

- Enabling us to use new channels and audiences to amplify our voice and increase brand awareness.
- Providing capacity build in the form of pro bono budget-relieving support and expertise.
- Providing new areas of insight and enabling different types of conversations with decision-makers.
- Providing broader resources for community impact, particularly where corporate employees have a natural concern.

There are many commercial organisations where customer care and social action activities, not strictly related to profitability, create a longer-term loyalty and value for the brand. In Shelter's case organisations dealing with home, financial services and most obviously construction would benefit from a collaborative partnership. Partnerships that deliver real impact can help the corporate to earn trust and respect from all its stakeholders.

Relationships take time to nurture and blossom and commitment from both sides to maintain. For both partners, this includes resources and, most importantly, common passion. The most successful corporate partnerships involve key ingredients:

- An alignment between the business strategy of both the charity and the company.
- The management of the charity relationship as a long-term business investment.
- Deep involvement of the CEO, executive directors and the Board on both sides.

Legal & General have been long-time supporters of Shelter, financially supporting Shelter services and research. An investment in safe and affordable housing is an important part of Legal & General's business model and by working in partnership we provide opportunities for each other to amplify our reach: e.g. Legal & General hosted Shelter's Round Table debate around housing; together we attend relevant exhibitions, introducing each other to new potential partners; Berkeley Group is a multi-year partner of Shelter, funding our services and working publicly alongside us to lift awareness of the critical role of housing in the economic recovery. In both of these examples, the alignment of mission and values is critical for both partners as it enables us to increase the resonance of our voice and reach, by pooling our expertise and position in our respective fields."

TOP TIP: "The key to the ideal partnership is to find activities that build the mission and values of both organisations. As with all successful relationships, it is an art and not a science and it requires trust and respect between each other in order to thrive."

SUMMARY

It pays to keep the romance alive

This process of weaving the corporate and charity more closely together results in pushing the relationship towards a much more strategic alliance that can endure for a longer period of time. The challenge is how to get to know each other in a way that promotes honest dialogue and builds trust.

The partnership should seek to:

- Create regular reviews
- Measure progress
- Report success
- Celebrate achievement
- Seek external recognition

TEN-POINT ACTION PLAN		
Action Point 1	Single	Know your purpose
Action Point 2	Dating	Create a compelling proposal
Action Point 3	Engaged	Agree a joint strategy
Action Point 4	Vows	Draw up a written agreement
Action Point 5	Honeymoon	Secure top-level commitment
Action Point 6	Marriage	Engage hearts and minds
Action Point 7	Benefits	Negotiate mutually beneficial terms
Action Point 8	**Date nights**	**Celebrate and recognise success** ✓

CHAPTER NINE

Beyond marriage

THE FORMAL PARTNERSHIP IS OFFICIALLY AT AN END – STAYING FRIENDS IS SO IMPORTANT

HOW DO YOU ACHIEVE THAT AMICABLE SEPARATION?

The models explored in this guide all had very different time-lines, ranging from the strict "Charity of the Year" to very long-term partnerships. Whichever model you are operating, it is important that you exit the partnership in a planned and professional way.

Strong partnerships rarely end with an absolute cut-off. On the contrary, lasting bonds are formed which create legacy opportunities and relationships that can be revisited.

The exit process is a critical event for ensuring a fantastic long lasting impression.

"Nomura was really proud to be able to step away from TCT knowing that the charity was strengthened in every way."

Anthony Harte,
Head of Community Affairs.
EMEA Nomura

"The legacy of giving for past partnerships contributes significantly to current revenue streams."

Maxine Trotter,
Director of Fundraising.
Help the Hospices

The sentiment from Anthony Harte is what all partnerships should aspire to. A partnership should aim to leave a stronger, better charity that can continue to go forward with new partners. Help the Hospices are experienced in partnership work and really value the importance of legacy income from corporate relationships.

FINDINGS:

Beyond Marriage – How to stay friends

What was interesting in all our case studies was how each partnership was either negotiated to endure beyond the original term or a relationship was maintained beyond the official end of the partnership. The charities with experience of partnership working persuaded their corporate partner to extend the partnership beyond one year. Two-three years seems an optimum time, depending on the size of the partnership.

The main reasons for planning a good ending are:

- The corporate wanting to leave the charity in a stronger position
- Completing the story and presenting a compelling case study
- Having a powerful message of thanks to colleagues helps to drive engagement
- Strong brand positioning and reputational value
- External recognition from awards
- Sharing learning in order to help the next partnership

Legacy value: The ending is all important with regards to leaving the door open for future collaboration, one-off advice and for legacy giving. Whizz-Kidz says it is as if they have never really left Tesco, they are still in regular contact and still receive help and advice. Help the Hospices partnership with Royal Mail Group ended in 2008, but they continue to receive approximately £17,000 each month from payroll-giving from Royal Mail colleagues who have never stopped caring about the partner they gave so much to.

Responsible exit: It is clear that corporates must avoid leaving a charity that is unprepared for a sudden departure. This is especially true if a large corporate is partnering a smaller charity. If there has been a successful partnership resulting in a big increase in funds, what will happen to the charity if this funding stream suddenly stops. Charities have to strike a balance between scaling up to capitalise on a partnership and being left over-staffed at the end. All of this should be planned for as the partnership progresses. Charities need to be robust in preparing for their exit strategy. If for any reason they might be left exposed or vulnerable then they must raise this with the corporate partner to see whether support can be given.

Change-over period: For the charity in particular, finding the next partner is critical and this new research needs to be balanced with celebrating the end of a current partnership. The parallel processes can become resource intensive and if possible you should have a team looking for new partners and a team managing existing partnerships.

Lasting friendship: Care should always be taken where personal relationships have been built, especially if this has resulted from volunteering or mentoring. The ending of an official partnering arrangement should not imply that all contact must cease. This process will have been all about engaging hearts and minds and if someone has really bought into a particular cause this should be helped to continue naturally.

Conclusion: In many cases a successful partnership ensures that the door is left open for the charity to return with a specific request for support at some point in the future. In a lot of cases, it is the CEO of the corporate partner who becomes instrumental in opening new avenues for the charity to pursue. CEOs have amazing networks and will invariably know someone at a company the charity is now trying to impress. References and introductions are a useful way of generating new partners.

CASE HISTORY

Argos and Help the Hospices planned their finale

The charity partnership between Argos and Help the Hospices was formed in July 2005 and had an agreement for two years. The partnership was a great success and raised over £1.2 million for hospice care.

Preparing for the end of the partnership in 2007 was always part of the partnership plan.

Primarily a fundraising partnership, Argos used cause-related marketing, employee fundraising initiatives as well as product sales to raise £1,236,461 for Help the Hospices – over twice the amount it had originally hoped for. From World Cup wristbands to reindeer food (standard recipe: magical oats and glitter!), Tick to Give schemes to engaging charity champions, the alliance with Help the Hospices was Argos's most successful charity partnership to date.

Help the Hospices believes a key factor behind the huge success of the partnership was its localised nature – every hospice was linked to one or more Argos stores in its local community. The benefit of this was that all the funds that were raised on a local level supported the communities that employees lived and worked in.

In preparing to wind down the partnership both teams ensured effective collaboration, communication and planning.

Both Argos and Help the Hospices stressed the importance of talking to each other at all stages of the partnership and even more so at the end.

In order to learn as much as they could from their experience with Help the Hospices, Argos also sent out employee questionnaires to gain a better understanding of how staff felt about the partnership. Communication with the community was done primarily though in-store advertising and local press.

Argos plans in six-month blocks and, as such, planning for the new charity partner began six months before the partnership with Help the Hospices came to an end, with the results of the employee vote on the new partner internally announced in the February of 2007. Both parties felt that planning – be it six or even three months in advance – ensured that everyone knew where they stood and was prepared when the partnership finally came to an end.

When Argos appointed their new charity partner and in order to make the transition for Argos as seamless as possible, Help the Hospices invited the account manager of Argos's new charity partner to spend some time with them. This really helped the incoming partner to plan the timing of their own communication process and learn first hand the finer details of the partnership.

Using Argos' and Help the Hospices' experiences has helped them both to derive some key points useful for any organisation nearing the end of a corporate-charity partnership:

TOP TIP: "Asking people from both organisations how they felt about the partnership once it has ended really helps you plan and share learning with the next partner."

Maxine Trotter,
Director of Fundraising.
Help the Hospices

- Start planning three to six months beforehand to ensure risks are minimised and opportunities are maximised.
- Ensure that communication channels with employees as well as the charity/company are always kept open.
- Don't cut off communication with your partner organisation the day the partnership ends: ongoing communication allows for a smoother transition.
- Continue to recognise achievements and milestones to keep the momentum of the partnership going until the very end.
- Celebrate the success of the partnership by applying for sector awards and provide updates for employees about how the money they have raised has been used.
- Ensure you have thanked all the people at the partner organisation for all the help they have provided, from the CEO to the employees raising the funds.

The two-year partnership between Help the Hospices and Argos is one that will not be easily forgotten by colleagues. There is still a great deal of mutual respect between the organisations with both showing support for the other.

While companies with deeper community involvement may face greater challenges in ending their charity partnerships than those faced by Argos, there are certainly lessons to be learnt from how amicably Help the Hospices and Argos parted ways.

ACTION POINT 9:

Start planning for the end of the partnership at least six months beforehand. Think about how you both want to feel about the partnership when it ends and work towards this.

Beyond Marriage – Forever friends

Celebrating the official ending of a partnership is really important as it helps people to feel proud of what has been achieved.

Help the Hospices has been working in partnership with Jones Lang LaSalle since 2009. Together they have raised £200,000 through a variety of activities. When the partnership was drawing to an end, Help the Hospices developed a six-month plan to ensure that all the final activities were supported, key individuals thanked and all aspects of the partnership were successfully drawn to a close.

The very nature of these charity-corporate relationships draws on the passion and enthusiasm of many individuals. Saying "thank you" is a vital part of ending a relationship. Plan how you are going to say thank you. The leadership of both organisations will have played a tremendous role in driving any partnership. Equally the thank-you process should start at the top.

A good way to end a partnership is with the publication of a case study, a video diary, a collection of stories or a more formal measure of success. However you chose to do this, it will be a critical part of your communications plan. People like being valued and thanked, whether it is a quiet moment of praise or a recognition award. Being proud of a collaborative achievement brings a great partnership to a good ending.

KPMG formed a two-year partnership in 2008 with the Alzheimer's Society. They reached a £1 million milestone within 23 months. Despite the partnership ending in 2010, both organisations remain proud of their achievements and many colleagues at KPMG remain connected to the charity.

It is important to recognise that the work of the charity doesn't stop just because a partnership has ended. The relationships that have been built up over the period of the partnership will, in many cases, want to continue naturally. A corporate would be wise not to stifle this employee passion and should allow it to continue.

If the public have been involved, then a clear communication plan is needed from the charity to thank them for their support. This is especially important as the charity may well be announcing another such partnership and will want to keep loyal donors.

SECRETS TO SUCCESS

Stronger for knowing you – planning to stay friends

As the benefits of corporate-charity partnerships are more widely recognised, so more will be sought. You probably won't be the first partner and you won't be the last. Fitting in neatly to an emerging cycle of events, handing over the baton to a new partner and starting a new relationship will all require careful planning.

Exercise:

How do you want to feel at the end of the partnership? It really helps to discuss how you want people to remember the partnership. If you are working towards a goal, are you going to achieve it? Six months from the end you should be well on track for success.

What kind of celebration is appropriate? Once you know the end date of your relationship you need to decide whether a celebratory party or a series of thank-you events is appropriate.

How will you position the communication process to facilitate a change in partner? You need to be careful on mixing the messages between celebrating an outgoing partnership and welcoming a new partner. Is it a straight handover date or a change-over period?

How will your external branding be affected? If you have delivered a customer-facing campaign, especially if this is centred on cause-related marketing or public giving how will you thank the public and how will you position a change in partner? You will need to factor into the budget the recall of any branded literature and change over of communications.

What kind of natural legacy relationships are likely to remain? Natural allegiances are created especially if the charity cause is close to the heart of an individual. Help the Hospices is particularly good at maintaining connections with individuals. Volunteering and mentoring programmes will also create bonds between individuals and the charity. It is important that these relationships are welcomed and enabled to continue.

How can a formal legacy relationship be managed? Many of the partnerships looked at in this guide talked about ongoing relationships. Creating a channel of communication that enables the charity to seek out support in the future is important. Making connections with the corporate's supply chain or customer base, providing testimonials or helping with future pitches are all ways in which a legacy relationship can be maintained.

What will you do if the partnership was not considered to be a great success? Not every corporate-charity partnership can be a fantastic success story. This poses a difficult challenge when presenting the final case study and press releases. The majority of partnerships will always have a degree of success and lessons to draw upon.

MICHAEL HOWARD (THE RT HON LORD HOWARD OF LYMPNE QC),

Chair of Help the Hospices
discusses the impact of the charity-corporate relationship and the importance of sustaining strong relationships

"All charitable causes are focussed on capturing the hearts and minds of people and enlisting support. This holds true for my own charity, Help the Hospices, the leading charity for hospice care. One in two people know a close friend or relative who has benefited from hospice care – with hospices helping 360,000 people affected by life-limiting and terminal illnesses each year. Collectively, hospices have to raise £1.5 million per day just to keep going. This makes hospice care the largest community fundraising cause in the UK.

The partnerships we have been privileged to work with include, KPMG, Royal Mail Group, Argos and many others. All of these partnerships help raise vital funds to support our work. These partnerships, however, are not just about the short-term fundraising, they are about sustaining long-term personal connections with people. Employers have access to large networks of people with whom we might not otherwise be able to communicate directly. We know that when people see first hand the services that hospices deliver for local communities that they will be proud to stay associated with our charity. Many of these relationships that are built during the partnership often continue long after the official ending of the partnership.

These connections enable charities to benefit from the long-term giving and support that continues after a partnership may have ended. For instance, payroll-giving, personal donations and volunteering all have the potential to continue long into the future. We believe that the strong personal connection that develops between an individual and their local hospice, stemming from an employer-led programme is a powerful connection process that truly touches the hearts and minds of individuals.

Raising awareness of hospice care is also an important aspect of our corporate partnerships. Letting employees know about the type of hospice services that are available can help dispel myths and fears around hospice care. It may be sometime into the future, long after a partnership has officially ended, that an individual may have need of their local hospice services. Corporate partnerships are a powerful way of informing large numbers of people about such services and ensuring that people know help is available should they need it.

Of course we are delighted when we secure a new corporate partner and a great deal of planning goes into the delivery of such a relationship. We are equally mindful to ensure that all of our partnership are successfully managed and reach their full potential."

TOP TIP:"One of the great benefits of corporate partnerships is having access to large numbers of people who have the potential to become long-term supporters of the charity. Maintaining these connections is vital."

SUMMARY

It's important to stay friends

Having successfully delivered an amazing partnership it is important to have an equally amazing ending. Celebrating success is important, but it is even more important to be able to end a partnership with the charity partner in a really strong position.

As the end approaches:

- Thank people for their fantastic support
- Prepare people for a change in partnership
- Support ongoing friendships
- Help the new partner
- Recognise achievements

A good ending is helped along by:

- Planning for the end at least six months in advance
- Knowing what success should feel like
- Legacy relationships
- An open door for future help and support
- A seamless handover to a new partner

The outcome should be:

- A stronger charity partner
- Colleagues who feel proud
- A great case study
- Recognition and PR for both partners
- A wider impact on society

TEN-POINT ACTION PLAN		
Action Point 1	Single	Know your purpose
Action Point 2	Dating	Create a compelling proposal
Action Point 3	Engaged	Agree a joint strategy
Action Point 4	Vows	Draw up a written agreement
Action Point 5	Honeymoon	Secure top-level commitment
Action Point 6	Marriage	Engage hearts and minds
Action Point 7	Benefits	Negotiate mutually beneficial terms
Action Point 8	Date nights	Celebrate and recognise success
Action Point 9	**Beyond marriage**	**Forever friends ✓**

CHAPTER TEN

Reflections

OFFICIALLY OVER – WHAT HAVE YOU LEARNT?

TAKE TIME TO REFLECT AND APPRECIATE THE MEMORIES.

We have seen from the examples of best practice in this guide that partnerships can take many forms and there is no single perfect model. Your past experience, however, can help shape your future performance.

Taking time to look back and reflect on the experience is the final step in managing the charity-corporate partnership

"I have had the privilege to be a part of several corporate-charity partnerships. My purpose in writing this guide is to reflect on those moments that really made a difference and share that learning with others. I hope by reading this guide that you will be inspired to push the boundaries of your own charity-corporate partnership."

Kay Allen OBE,
Director.
Diverse Advice Ltd

FINDINGS:

Reflections – what lessons have been learnt?

Honest feedback: Taking the time to reflect formally on the partnership enables honest feedback to be given to both partners, without fear of damaging any key relationships. Feedback is an important part of the learning process and will help both partners to improve on future relationships.

Wider success: Sometimes it is only after the formal relationship has ended that you can really sum up the value of the partnership. The opportunity for external recognition from awards may in fact happen sometime after the formal ending of the partnership.

Unexpected success: Having the time to reflect on every aspect of the partnership can often reveal moments of unexpected success.

Maintaining contact: It is important that strong links are maintained once the official partnership is over. You will have built up a great deal of knowledge that can continue to add value long into the future.

Unicef and Proctor & Gamble recently announced that their "one pack = one vaccine" campaign had raised the money to buy 300 million vaccines against maternal neonatal tetanus. The sheer magnitude of this achievement and the possibility of eliminating this disease bring into sharp relief the true power of charity-corporate partnerships. This fantastic partnership grew out of a courtship process between colleagues at Unicef and Proctor & Gamble.

CASE HISTORY

Linklaters and Camfed reflect on their partnership from 2007 to 2011

Linklaters supports its clients in achieving their strategies across emerging and developed markets around the world. It uses its expertise and resources to help the world's leading organisations pursue opportunities and manage risk wherever it does business.

The firm's long-established community investment programme aims to provide a similar quality of support to disadvantaged communities local to their 27 offices around the world as well as in regions where its expertise can support the Millennium Development Goals (MDGs). Linklaters assigns 0.5% of global pre-tax profits to charitable donations annually and contributes the equivalent of another 0.5% in pro bono time and volunteering.

Camfed – the Campaign for Female Education – was launched in 1993 with the mission to deliver girls' education and the empowerment of young women as the route to lasting social change in sub-Saharan Africa. To date, Camfed has successfully supported the education of more than 1,400,000 children in five countries, and is rapidly expanding. Linklaters' and Camfed's story and success clearly reflects our Ten-Point Action Plan.

A courtship:
Camfed and Linklaters were first introduced in 2007. The nature of any collaboration was at this stage unknown and so early conversations were about mutual understanding and trust. Over time, these developed into a much deeper appreciation of strengths, opportunities and, therefore, synergy. Only at this point did governance become the obvious focus for the partnership and from here both organisations established clear objectives for their participation.

Developing a compelling proposition:
Linklaters had a clear vision for a new global, charity partnership. The firm wanted an opportunity which would make use of its skills and expertise in addressing the achievement of one or more of the MDGs, preferably with international relevance. A further purpose and benefit of such a partnership comes through colleagues gaining valuable experience and, where appropriate, opportunities for client collaboration. A charity partnership provides a common purpose to structure the delivery of such work, ensuring that impact is effective and enabling the full participation of all those involved.

Camfed wanted to explore the importance of governance in aid and relief work, by initially investigating their own model throughout their international activity. They were interested in having lawyers apply their perspective and expertise to these issues. Over time, their motivation extended to include not just internal review but, ambitiously, to generate debate around standards for governance in the international development sector. This is an important international affairs issue and a crucial element of how the sector delivers its work. Camfed needed a professional and robust report on which to base their advocacy.

TOP TIP: "Asking people from both organisations how they felt about the partnership once it has ended really helps you plan and share learning with the next partner."

Maxine Trotter,
Director of Fundraising.
Help the Hospices

A joint strategy was agreed:
Camfed already had great confidence in their model and this gave them confidence in the partnership. The charity believed in its approach and so was confident to work with Linklaters in an honest and professional manner. This commitment to openness was of critical importance to Linklaters, for whom anything less would not have permitted full analysis. Together the two organisations developed a two-year plan of action. This included clear information-sharing and agreement as to the purpose and merit of the partnership. It ensured that the partnership would deliver both sides' objectives whilst also contributing to a broader debate on international aid.

Leadership:
To ensure high-profile leadership and management of the project, two senior Linklaters partners (one each from the UK and the US) led the scoping of the partnership with the CEO and Deputy CEO of Camfed. Working across sectors and borders was initially challenging: different cultures, norms and attitudes led to occasional misunderstanding and confusion. As the partnership grew, these differences were understood and appreciated for the new perspectives which they brought. The process and product were strengthened as a result.

Engaged hearts and minds:
Uniquely, the partnership work included three field trips to sub-Saharan Africa and resulted in over 3,500 hours of pro bono work by 20 lawyers at Linklaters. Opening their entire operations to ground-level scrutiny was a brave step by Camfed. In particular, allowing "outsiders" to speak to valued project partners and beneficiaries demanded a high degree of trust and integrity, something which would have been impossible without the foundation of a robust partnership.

The Linklaters' lawyers gained a great deal from the experience of working with Camfed in Africa and formed close bonds with the charity. Their growing understanding of how they were contributing to Camfed's future success was a turning point in the partnership. Translating this into firm-wide communication sparked the imagination of Linklaters' people back in the offices, for whom this had initially seemed a puzzling collaboration. As a result, interest in the project extended beyond the original participants to much broader engagement: a development process seen as hugely positive.

The benefits of the partnership:
In connection with the project, Linklaters contributed £200,000 to Camfed to enable 433 girls across Zimbabwe, Ghana, Zambia, Tanzania and Malawi to receive their full four years of secondary-school education. Building on the report, the firm has also identified an opportunity to take the governance theme to a wider audience and is now focusing on applying and developing the lessons learnt by its analysis of the Camfed model. Camfed is using the report to enhance the way it looks at and delivers governance and

TOP TIP: "The true value of a partnership will emerge over time as you establish ways of working together. It is important to look back on these moments and capture lessons learned in order to improve your capacity for future partnership work."

Matthew Sparkes,
Global Head of Corporate Responsibility,
Linklaters

accountability to its clients – girls and young women in Africa. Both institutions are working to bring the issue of governance to the forefront within the sector, taking the work forward together rather than separately.

A good ending:
Following the research phase, both organisations admit to underestimating the time required to ensure that the published report would be accessible to a wide range of audiences. The need to blend theory with practice demanded equal input from both sides and this took time, understanding and much revision. Again, mutual respect allowed for robust debate which resulted in a stronger analysis and, most importantly, a better report. "Accounting to the Girl" was subsequently launched on 14 April 2010 at the opening plenary of the Skoll World Forum – the pre-eminent annual global gathering of social investors and entrepreneurs – in Oxford.

The project has been so successful that a second phase of pro bono work was announced in September 2010. Linklaters and Camfed announced a joint commitment to action as part of their participation at the Clinton Global Initiative annual meeting in New York. This second phase of pro bono work will continue to champion issues of governance, transparency and accountability, particularly in relation to international aid.

Recognition:
Both organisations have also used the partnership and its results to position themselves within their respective sectors as thematic experts on global governance; being recognised at the Clinton Global Initiative added enormous credibility in this respect. This is reflected most recently by Camfed and Linklaters being founding partners of a new "Advancing Good Governance in International Development" conference at Oxford University.

Reflections:
Dependent on pro bono support, the context of this partnership differs from other case studies looked at in this guide. Its story illustrates that the mechanics for managing a good relationship is the same no matter what the purpose or style or, indeed, the outcome. In fact, it is clear that in a new phase of the partnership, the two organisations are moving forward together in some areas but in differing directions elsewhere. This again underlines the strength of the partnership.

Linklaters and Camfed's story eloquently illustrates the steps through which a partnership should work. Not without its challenges, the honesty and professionalism reflected in their case study is what ultimately underpinned their success and overcame potentially difficult moments.

ACTION POINT 10:

Once the partnership has ended set aside time to reflect on the whole of the partnership journey. Challenge your own performance and behaviour to ensure you are working in the best way possible.

Reflections – Lessons learned

Every organisation is different and so every partnership will have different aims and objectives. Successes will have been measured and recognised throughout the partnership as objectives are delivered. It is just as important, however, to take the time to reflect on the partnership as a whole.

It is important to identify and reflect upon both moments of excitement and moments of frustration. Identify what you could do differently second time around.

Use feedback mechanisms to hear directly from those involved in delivering activities to understand what worked well. If possible, survey customers and third parties who were connected with the partnership to seek their views.

All partnerships will have some measure of success. The bigger questions that can now be reviewed are did the partnership add value to the objectives of both organisations and did it make a difference to the cause it was addressing?

B&Q's partnership with UK Youth and Youth Work Ireland focuses on skills delivery to youth groups around the country. A Youth Can Do It Grant has been launched which links each of the 330 stores to local youth groups for a three-year partnership. B&Q is focusing on enhancing the skills of young people using the company's expertise in DIY to help make a difference to the local community. The driving force behind this initiative was recognition that the younger generation is not inheriting DIY skills in the way previous generations did, and therefore the community programme aims to help bridge this skills gap. There is a clear connection between a need in the community and a longer-term business benefit to B&Q.

Charity-corporate partnerships are about creating legacies to be proud of so ensure you have a mechanism for capturing the total impact of what was achieved.

Each partnership is unique but lessons and experiences are transferable. Use the experience to improve on future partnerships.

Sharing the journey in an honest case study will inspire other organisations to seek out the powerful connection of a charity-corporate collaboration.

SECRETS TO SUCCESS

Fond memories or regrets – learn from past experiences

Capture those moments that made a difference and that sparked real momentum in a relationship. Taking time to reflect on what has happened is often overlooked as we become caught up in the business of today.

Exercise:

Set aside some time to look back on the partnership and reflect on the ten steps set out in this guide:

1. In choosing the partner, were you clear on what you were looking for?
2. Was the proposal and decision-making process compelling and transparent?
3. Were synergies discovered and was the joint aim clear?
4. Was the agreement robust enough and did it adequately cover the partnership?
5. Was the leadership and management structure strong and purposeful?
6. How well did you engage people across both organisations?
7. Was the true value of the partnership recognised, measured and celebrated?
8. Was the review process sufficient, did you capture enough information?
9. Was there a good ending, have you been able to sustain contact for the future?
10. Having had time to reflect – what knowledge has been acquired?

A simple four-stage process of challenging yourself:

What went well?

What helped the partnership to move forward? What seemed to facilitate positive effects?

What didn't go well?

What restricted the partnership, were there any obstacles that prevented projects from delivering to their full potential?

What would you change/do differently next time?

There are always moments that you wish had gone differently, have you acknowledged the lessons from these?

What feedback have you had from colleagues/customers/ clients of the charity?

Feedback is a valuable source of information that challenges your own perspective.

CAROLINE WATERS, OBE

Director of People and Policy
reflects on why BT values its relationships with charity partners

"Partnerships create opportunities to support our people to do the things they are passionate about in their local communities – for BT that means all one hundred thousand of them. Our purpose is to partner with charities that represent the issues that BT are passionate about and that we can throw our voice behind, e.g. Childline and Digital Inclusion. A proposal that sees each other's point of view is essential. There will always be a win/win, the skill is to identify how to get the most from a partnership.

A shared sense of purpose develops when there are common passions and aspirations. Finding a compatible partner is important. Have fun experimenting and testing the boundaries and then commit to a jointly developed proposition where each partner knows what their role is, but which offers room to be influenced by both as it evolves. Agreeing a partnership needs a degree of formality and a clear picture of who does what best. Having clearly agreed expectations and role clarity from the start is a must, but don't be too rigid. Everything should be flexible and responsive to any opportunities that arise. I'd certainly go for early clarity but don't think about exit too soon – after all, who plans for divorce?

Leadership is essential if everyone is to share vision. Role clarity must be established so that each partner focuses on what they do best. Good governance provides review opportunities and ensures harmony is maintained until the job is done. Despite clarity and compatibility, things can still go awry – usually when people stop talking or issues go unvoiced. Keep focused on the outcome and how you will work together to overcome whatever is thrown at you. Partnerships fail when organisations cease to build and review together. If you feel this happening – call it out. Use a facilitator because it helps you see the problem and not apportion blame. Giving each partner the freedom to get on with what they do best in a conversational environment really works and is characterised by efficiency, effectiveness and productivity – it's all about making the whole bigger than the sum of the parts.

Most relationships start with great energy and curiosity; maintaining it is tough when it gets down to the daily grind of living together. Build in opportunities to be creative, to brainstorm and challenge. Don't rely on formality but keep the partnership going by learning about why each partner cares about the outcome.

Partnerships end best when they did what they set out to do. That means building in flexibility; not losing sight of the end game or throwing it away because of a deadline that has become irrelevant. It's what you achieve together that matters – never forget that and you will create legacies to be proud of. Each partnership is unique; but the governance, clarity and excitement that made it effective and enjoyable is transferrable. Use each experience to hone your contribution, spark new skills and develop a reputation that says you will hold up your end of the deal. An honest partner open to learning and challenge will never want for great partners."

TOP TIP: "Employees can be passionate advocates for a business. Helping colleagues to get involved with issues they are passionate about brings added value back to the company, builds employee loyalty and a brand that is respected and trusted by customers."

THE ULTIMATE ACTION PLAN

We have now worked through every stage of our Ten-Point Action Plan to help you realise the potential you have to be a great partner

1. SINGLE? Think through the purpose for wanting a charity-corporate partnership. Be clear on your own values and ethics. Make sure you **Know your purpose**.
2. DATING? Research your potential partner, ensure due diligence, identify synergies and potential benefits and present the proposition as a win/win scenario. Make sure you **Create a compelling proposal**.
3. ENGAGED. Get to know each other. A partnership must be based on honesty and trust and the ability to listen to one another. Work together to **Agree a joint strategy**.
4. VOWS. A contract sets the parameters of the partnership and provides a safety net for both. Get the ground rules laid down and **Draw up a written agreement**.
5. HONEYMOON. Visible senior leadership sets the tone of the relationship and a strong management structure delivers the day-to-day running of the partnership. Make sure you **Secure top-level commitment**.
6. MARRIAGE. Success is predicated on engaging people with the partnership – managing the ups and downs – generating new ideas – all relationships need give and take. **Engage hearts and minds**.
7. BENEFITS. Understand the value that both partners bring and that this is a two-way process. **Negotiate mutually beneficial terms**.
8. DATE NIGHTS. Sustaining passion and enthusiasm for the partnership helps deliver long-term impact make sure you **Celebrate and recognise success**.
9. BEYOND MARRIAGE. Preparing for the official ending of the partnership can ensure a healthy productive relationship is maintained so that you can stay **Forever friends**.
10. REFLECTIONS. Take time to prepare for the next relationship and hand over to the incoming partner. **Lessons learned**.

CONCLUSION

"Throughout my career I have had the privilege of working for a few of the most respected brands in the UK, including B&Q, BSkyB, Royal Mail Group and Fujitsu.

I have seen first-hand that a business that operates ethically has an integrity that permeates throughout the organisation.

At B&Q, for example, there is certainly no evidence of 'green-washing' in its approach to sustainability. Their approach to inclusive employment for older people has endured changes of leadership and key personnel and yet it still remains a flagship policy. B&Q recognises that it draws its profits from the communities where they operate and it seems to know instinctively that being a good neighbour is synonymous with being a good and profitable business. Equally, Marks & Spencer, when they launched Plan A, had this as part of the way they do business and they are starting to monetise the benefits back to their bottom line.

I passionately believe that corporate responsibility can sit comfortably within the profit model and I believe that the rise in consumer knowledge and power to act will force many more corporates to behave more responsibly. Being a good company will not depend just on having an effective CR department, but it will become a way of doing business, expected and demanded by stakeholders.

The CEO is, in my experience, critical to driving this attitude towards good business. Philip N Green, Sir Stuart Rose, Adam Crozier, Ian Cheshire, Paul Dreschler and many more are all CEOs who have delivered profitable companies within a powerful framework of being a responsible business.

The corporate-charity partnership is just one element of how a business can work towards a positive social impact and this guide has a narrow focus on how to leverage the power of partnerships. As the funding model for many charities starts to change, corporates will have a more central role in collaborative working to enable the third sector to deliver.

I believe we will see a trend towards greater collaboration and smarter partnerships. The more traditional 'Charity of the Year' may always have a place, but the true value of corporate-charity partnerships will come from stronger strategic alliances, over longer periods of time, that are not afraid to tackle difficult social problems affecting communities. Charities have a new opportunity to seek out innovative partnership models and should take up this challenge.

Businesses need healthy communities to help their businesses thrive and the charities have the expertise to help tackle some of our deepest social problems. Together corporates and charities can be a powerful change agent for good – providing each seeks to understand the other's point of view.

I have faith that harnessing the power of the charity-corporate partnership will lead to greater social good."

Kay Allen

INDEX – KEY WORD SEARCH

About the authors: Kay Allen and Tanja Rasmussen are two like-minded individuals who have voluntarily come together to create this best practice guide. Both have witnessed the benefits of an effective partnership but have also seen some challenges and missed opportunities. Both have a sense that the days of "cheque book charity" are gone as corporates demand more from their charity relationships.

Kay Allen

Kay Allen is Director of Every Business Commits, a campaign that aims to encourage business to support local communities, driving greater social responsibility. A career that includes Royal Mail Group, BSkyB and B&Q, her work has focused on Equality and Social Action. Kay has served as a Commissioner on both the Disability Rights Commission and the Equality and Human Rights Commission. She also served as a Non-Executive Director of the Pension and Disability Carers Service. She has 20 years' experience in supporting strategic partnerships between corporates and charities looking for innovative solutions that have a positive impact on society. Kay also runs her own consultancy and has a number of clients whom she advises on CR. Kay is an accredited coach to EMCC and was awarded an OBE in 2011.

Tanja Rasmussen

Tanja Rasmussen is Programme Director for Knighton White, and before that spent four years as Partnership & Community Investment Director for Business in the Community. Her work focuses on increasing the positive impact of companies on society, by promoting innovation, strategic integration and development, and cross-sector partnerships. Tanja has worked closely with the government and strategic voluntary sector partners on key community issues – she led the taskforce on the UK recession response to communities most at risk. Previously, Tanja was the Community Affairs Manager for Microsoft UK, leading their charity partnerships and focusing on issues of employability and education. Originally from Denmark, Tanja holds a Research Master in Social Anthropology.

Their perspective explores the similarities between the corporate-charity partnership and that of a marriage, from dating, getting engaged and living together to an amicable separation, offering key insights and top tips for success.

USEFUL ADDRESSES FOR FURTHER ADVICE

Kay Allen
Diverse Advice Ltd

Diverse Advice Ltd provides bespoke consultancy and advice to corporates and charities helping them to leverage the most from responsible business practices. Coaching is offered to support individuals/teams through the development of CR practices and corporate-charity partnerships.

Tel: 07826 926313
Email: kay.allen@diverseadvice.com
Website: www.diverseadvice.com
Twitter @fasood

Brandanomics

Positive impact is the third fundamental economic dimension that creates profitable and flourishing brands. A business model that relies solely on supply and demand is unsustainable: a product or service must be more than price and quantity. By looking at the elasticity of supply and demand coupled with addressing a brand's impact curve, Brandanomics positions organisations to be the businesses of tomorrow, fine-tuned and forward-thinking, and creates brands as currencies to be respected, emulated and traded.

South Wing
Somerset House
Strand
London WC2R 1LA
Tel: 020 7845 5840
Email: earth@beyondbranding.co.uk
Website: www.beyondbranding.co.uk

Business in the Community

BITC is a membership organisation of over 850 companies, with engagement in 10,700 organisations internationally and an employee reach of 14.7 million, Business in the Community is raising the benchmark for responsible business practice. They offer members practical support to help them transform their businesses and integrate responsible practices into their operations. Business in the Community is one of Prince Charles' charities, a group of not-for-profit organisations of which The Prince of Wales is President.

Business in the Community
137 Shepherdess Walk
London N1 7RQ
Tel: 020 7566 8650
Email: information@bitc.org.uk
Twitter: @BITC1
Website: www.bitc.org.uk.

Charity Retail Association

The Charity Retail Association (CRA) is a member organisation dedicated to supporting registered charities that run shops as part of their fundraising activities. It has developed a code of charity retailing that is mandatory for its members. The CRA does not provide legal advice or guidance to individuals enquiring about setting up a charity shop.

Charity Retail Association
Central House
14 Upper Woburn Place
London WC1H 0AE
Tel: 020 7255 4470
Email: mail@charityretail.org.uk
Website: www.charityretail.org.uk

USEFUL ADDRESSES FOR FURTHER ADVICE

Charities Aid Foundation
The Charities Aid Foundation (CAF) supports charities in raising money and making that money go further. It provides information on tax-efficient giving and managing donations. Its website contains useful information, including details of new ways of raising funds.

Charities Aid Foundation
25 Kings Hill Avenue
Kings Hill
West Malling
Kent ME19 4TA
Tel: 03000 123 000
Email: enquiries@cafonline.org
Website: www.cafonline.org

CST The GATE
CST The Gate is a fully integrated advertising agency specialising in the charity sector. With clients such as The Royal British Legion, Diabetes UK, Arthritis Care and many others, they can answer any charity's needs in terms of branding, building awareness, fundraising, on and off line advertising, social media activity, website design and build and media strategy, planning and buying.

CST The Gate
Devon House
58 St Katharine's Way
London E1W 1LB
Tel: 020 7423 4500
Email: simon.rowley@cstthegate.com
Website: www.cstthegate.com
Twitter: @cstthegate

Directory of Social Change
The Directory of Social Change (DSC) provides training and information to the voluntary and community sectors. Its charity centre in London has a small in-house reference library. The library includes over 1,000 books, reports and leaflets, including up-to-date funding guides.

Directory of Social Change
24 Stephenson Way
London NW1 2DP
Tel: 08450 777707
Email: enquiries@dsc.org.uk
Website: www.dsc.org.uk

Fundraising Standards Board
The Fundraising Standards Board (FRSB) is an independent complaints handling body that has been established to operate the public-facing side of self-regulation of fundraising. The FRSB encourages charities and fundraisers to become members of their self-regulation scheme and abide by the Institute's Codes of Fundraising Practice to ensure that each member commits to the highest fundraising standards and they have robust procedures in place. The FRSB investigates complaints from the public about the fundraising methods of its members if an unsatisfactory response has been received to an initial complaint made directly to the charity by a member of the public.

Fundraising Standards Board
61 London Fruit Exchange
Brushfield Street
London E1 6EP
Tel: 0845 402 5442
Email: info@frsb.org.uk
Website: www.frsb.org.uk

USEFUL ADDRESSES FOR FURTHER ADVICE

GoodPeople

GoodPeople's technology helps corporates, SMEs, or any "talent community":

1. to map their available skills and expertise
2. by brokering relationships directly with Civil Society organisations within the GoodPeople.co.uk network.

From virtual volunteering opportunities, to skills-based, longer-term volunteering relationships, GoodPeople makes connections between the talent pools of people who want to volunteer or offer pro bono support and the opportunity pools that exists in charities and social enterprises. If you need to find support for your social enterprise, or are looking to offer your expertise, GoodPeople can help you make the right connections.

Richard Tyrie
Tel: 07884 250985
Email: richard@goodpeople.co.uk
www.goodpeople.co.uk

Institute of Fundraising

The Institute of Fundraising (IoF) is the professional membership body for fundraising. Its mission is to support fundraisers, through leadership, representation, standards-setting and education.

The IoF website is a useful source of information, with specialised guidance on fundraising methods, standard fundraising agreements for charities and other information.

Institute of Fundraising
Park Place
12 Lawn Lane
London SW8 1UD
Tel: 020 7840 1000
Email: info@institute-of-fundraising.org.uk
Website: www.institute-of-fundraising.org.uk

HM Revenue & Customs

HM Revenue & Customs (HMRC) has a quick link for charities on the first page of its website. On the website you can access a wide range of guidance material for charities. Information includes details of VAT and tax issues for charities, including Gift Aid. HMRC has an email enquiry service and helpline.

HMRC Charities
St Johns House
Merton Road
Liverpool L75 1BB
Tel: 0845 302 0203 (8am-5pm Monday to Friday)
Email: charities@hmrc.gov.uk
Website: www.hmrc.gov.uk

USEFUL ADDRESSES FOR FURTHER ADVICE

Knighton White

Knighton White promotes leading philanthropy activity across all aspects of advice, project development and programme delivery. Experienced advisory and management services are offered to support businesses, charitable foundations, fund advisors, other professional advisors and individuals.

Tanja Rasmussen
Tel: 07843 780244
Email: tr@knightonwhite.com
Website: www.knightonwhite.com

National Association for Voluntary and Community Action

The National Association for Voluntary and Community Action (NAVCA) is the national voice of local voluntary and community sector infrastructure in England. Its purpose is to promote local voluntary and community action nationally. It does this through 360 local infrastructure organisations that provide a wide range of support, development and representation services to the local voluntary and community sector.

NAVCA
The Tower
2 Furnival Square
Sheffield S1 4QL
Tel: 0114 278 6636
Email: navca@navca.org.uk
Website: www.navca.org.uk

National Council for Voluntary Organisations

The National Council for Voluntary Organisations (NCVO) is the umbrella body for the voluntary and community sector in England. Its website includes information about funding, including an introduction to fundraising. The NCVO Helpdesk is a free service that provides advice and support for anyone involved in the voluntary sector.

National Council for Voluntary Organisations
Regents Wharf
8 All Saints Street
London N1 9RL
Tel: 0800 2798 798
Textphone: 0800 01 88 111 (Mincom)
Email: helpdesk@askncvo.org.uk
Website: www.ncvo-vol.org.uk

Office for Civil Society

The Office for Civil Society has developed guidance about what information must be provided to the public from professional fundraisers and commercial participators when they undertake a public collection on behalf of a charity.

Office for Civil Society
2nd Floor
Admiralty Arch
South Side The Mall
London SW1A 2WH
Tel: 020 7276 6400
Website: www.cabinetoffice.gov.uk

USEFUL ADDRESSES FOR FURTHER ADVICE

Public Fundraising Regulatory Association
The Public Fundraising Regulatory Association (PFRA) focuses specifically on face-to-face fundraising. Face-to-face fundraisers ask people to sign up to regular direct debit donations to charities. The PFRA is a membership organisation whereby members follow a code of practice for face-to-face fundraisers. The PFRA also provides some useful information for the public and trustees on its website.

Public Fundraising Regulatory Association
Unit 11, Europoint
5-11 Lavington Street
London SE1 0NZ
Tel: 020 7401 8452
Email: info@pfra.org.uk
Website: www.pfra.org.uk

The Cranfield Trust
The Cranfield Trust is a leading provider of free management consultancy to voluntary sector organisations in the social welfare field, specifically those addressing issues of poverty, disability and social exclusion. With a register of over 650 commercial sector volunteers, many of whom are alumni of business schools, as well as members of professional bodies, we provide tailored management consultancy projects to more than 250 voluntary organisations a year.

Cranfield Trust volunteers provide support on a range of issues including strategic and business planning, financial management, marketing, IT and human resources as well as acting as mentors and advisorsto charity Chief Executives and Boards. Our free online advice service, HRNet, offers specialist advice on employment issues.

The Cranfield Trust
Court Room Chambers
1 Bell Street
Romsey
Hampshire SO51 8GY

Tel: 01794 830338

email: admin@cranfieldtrust.org

www.cranfieldtrust.org

Wales Council for Voluntary Action
The Wales Council for Voluntary Action is the voice of the voluntary sector in Wales.

Wales Council for Voluntary Action
Baltic House
Mount Stuart Square
Cardiff Bay
Cardiff CF10 5 FH
Tel: 029 2043 1700
Bilingual Helpdesk: 0800 2888 329
Minicom: 02920431703
Email: help@wcva.org.uk
Website: www.wcva.org.uk

Drawing on research into ten successful corporate-charity partnerships, "Corporates are from Mars, Charities are from Venus: the Ultimate Guide Action Plan to Managing your Partnership" offers a framework for charities and corporate organisations to help leverage the most value from collaboration.

Using real case histories and expert opinions, and following a ten-step process, it demonstrates how to develop a systematic approach to any charity-corporate partnership. Good planning and honest communication are all essential elements that lead to success.

This guide is offered as a free resource. A donation of the cost price of £14.99 to our charity partner, Action for M.E., would be welcomed by the authors.

Their perspective explores the similarities between the corporate-charity partnership and that of a marriage, from dating, getting engaged and living together to an amicable separation, offering key insights and top tips for success.